Published in the UK in 2
The Stannah Grou
Watt Close, East Por
Andover, Hampshire SP

ISBN: 978-178578-3

Text copyright © 2018 Peter Pugh, B

Typeset in Classical Garamond

CONTENTS

PETER PUGH was educated at Oundle and Cambridge where he read History. He began his business career with Gillette and in 1984 began to write company histories. He has now written over 60 books on such companies as Rolls-Royce, for whom he wrote a three-volume history, De La Rue, Iceland Frozen Foods and United Biscuits. He wrote a book on the Guinness Scandal, an insider's guide to the City, and guides to the philosophy of Maynard Keynes and the legacy of Margaret Thatcher in the well-known *Introducing* series. He also wrote books on golf, including *Creating Classics*, *Masters of Design* and *The Ryder Cup*.

INTRODUCTION

In the year 2017 the Stannah family business has been providing for the family for some 150 years. Much of what has gone on has been lost forever. Without this record, it is probable that what is recorded within these pages would have gone the same way. That would be a tragedy. The present and future Stannah family members and the staff of the company will, we feel, wish to know the heritage of the family and its business and maybe gain pride and a sense of ownership of that history. For they are all part of it, that special something: 'a family business'.

In 2017 seven members of the family, two fourth-generation aged 82 and 78 and five fifth-generation aged between 52 and 42, lead the business, together with key non-family members of the Group Management Team. The top Board has for many years comprised about half family and half non-family Directors.

'The Book' (of which this is the introduction) attempts to chart the Stannah Lifts history with family records to add perspective from the beginning in the mid-1800s to now. Now is 2017 and the business operations are focused on lifts and stairlifts, with revenues of about £236 million and employing 1,900 people. The main products are lifts, stairlifts, escalators and walkways and related engineering and support, with nationwide UK coverage and subsidiaries in twelve countries and over 30 Distributorships around the world. The overseas business is mainly derived through stairlift sales.

Of the present generation, we, Brian and Alan, recall our father Leslie N. Stannah, known affectionately by family and staff alike as 'Pop', heading a small team in the 1950s of some 24 staff. He was the third generation, but also in a sense the founder of today's business, as his inheritance, on leaving the RNVR in 1945, was a pile of bricks; all that remained of the pre-war Stannah business after devastation by a German bomb.

This tale, therefore, is the sketchy history pre-Second World War and the achievements thereafter to the present. One wonders what the future holds.

Brian Stannah
Alan Stannah

AUTHOR'S ACKNOWLEDGEMENTS

It would be invidious to try to mention all the people I have interviewed in researching this book about the Stannah family business. Inevitably, I would miss someone. Nevertheless, I would like to thank all of them for their contributions, and those who sent in documents, letters, photographs and archives. I have quoted many of them in the text and that is an acknowledgement in itself.

I would like to mention three people without whom the book could not have been written. The first two are Brian and Alan Stannah who provided a great deal of information, written material and photographs and who patiently and meticulously amended the drafts. The third is Jocelyn Sharpe who acts as an Assistant to the two brothers. Joss has been unfailingly helpful and is a joy to work with. There is no question: this book could not have been completed without her help.

Peter Pugh
2017

i. Jocelyn Sharpe with her two bosses, Brian and Alan Stannah, whom she has served with dedication and efficiency for over 30 years. She has also contributed enormously to this history.

Peter Pugh wrote to me in 2006 offering his services as a writer of company histories. I recognised his name as the author of *The Magic of a Name* – a history of Rolls-Royce in three volumes published in 2002. Because so much of our company's history between the First World War and the Second World War is lost, we had wanted to get what is still known together with more recent events recorded for future generations. Here was the catalyst to do it. It has not been easy and has taken much longer than we expected. The problems we encountered were two-fold.

Peter wrote the first draft up to what was in 2011 the present, having conducted many interviews with family and staff. The result was the recording of past history as hoped for, together with a much more detailed account of activities from about 1987 with many contributions from folk all across the company. Alan felt strongly that this recent material made the whole unbalanced and that if written say a generation later would provide a truer picture of the key events and people's contributions. This has eventually resulted in the final chapter becoming a snapshot of the last 30 years in the briefest of detail, with the exception of a couple of highlights covered more fully.

The second issue was family content. The initial intention was to get the known company history recorded. In the beginning it was appropriate to base the early material on the family who start the tale. Thereafter, it has seemed appropriate to keep an eye on the doings of the family members up to the present to the extent that the book has now become a history of the Stannah family and their business. So be it. We hope future generations will be appreciative and that other readers will forgive us.

Brian Stannah

MONETARY VALUES

Money and its value is always a problem when writing about a period that stretches for more than 150 years, particularly when parts of that period have included some years of very high inflation. Furthermore, establishing a yardstick for measuring the change in the value of money is not easy either. Do we take the external value of the pound or what it will buy in the average, whatever that may be, weekly shopping basket? Do we relate it to the average manual wage? As we know, while prices in general might rise, and have done so in this country every year since the Second World War, the prices of certain products might fall. However, we are writing about a business, and money and its value crop up on almost every page. We therefore have to make some judgements. We can only generalise and I think the best yardstick is probably the average working wage.

Taking this as the yardstick, here is a measure of the pound sterling relative to the pound in 2017:

> 1837–1900 multiply by 120
> 1900–1914 multiply by 110

Apart from wartime, prices were stable for 250 years but prices began to rise in the run-up to the First World War.

To bring prices up to 2017 equivalents:

> 1918–1939 multiply by 60
> 1945–1950 multiply by 35
> 1950–1960 multiply by 30
> 1960–1970 multiply by 25
> 1970–1974 multiply by 20
> 1975–1977 multiply by 15

> 1978–1980 multiply by 8
> 1980–1987 multiply by 5
> 1987–1991 multiply by 2.5
> 1991–1997 multiply by 2
> 1997–2010 multiply by 1.5

Since 2010, the rate of inflation, by the standards of most of the twentieth century, has been very low, averaging, until very recently, less than the 1997–2010 Labour government's originally stated aim of 2.5 per cent (since reduced to 2 per cent). You don't need me to tell you that some things such as telephone charges and many items made in the Far East, notably China, can go down in price while others, such as houses, have moved up very sharply from 1997 to 2017.

CHAPTER ONE

1800–1900

JOSEPH STANNAH, AN INVENTIVE MAN

STANNAH HAS ALWAYS MADE THINGS

This is a great success story.

The Stannah family business in 2017 celebrated 150 years, with roots extending back another twenty, as you will see. It is not a business built overnight and not one built on sand. One could argue that the true foundation of the business started with the birth of Joseph Stannah in 1836, who was to become an extremely able and inventive engineer.

If your name is Stannah, lifts are in your blood. Every adult male Stannah since Joseph has worked in the lift industry if not in the family business. The son of Joseph, Albert Joseph – A.J. – had two sons, Leslie and Colin. Leslie, who became universally known as 'Pop', did not initially work in his father's firm, though he did work between the wars in the lift industry, both in the USA and in this country. Colin, the younger son, went to seek his fortune in Africa but even he could not resist the call of the lift industry and eventually became Managing Director and Chairman of Otis East Africa.

Albert Joseph himself had to contend with a very difficult period in Britain's, and indeed the world's, economic history. The First World War was clearly not helpful to the domestic construction industry, the 1920s was a poor decade for Britain and the 1930s was a disastrous period for almost the whole world. This was, of course, followed by yet another world war in which the Stannah factory was bombed out of existence.

Pop Stannah, showing the traditional family determination, built up the family business again from scratch and his two sons, Brian and Alan, built it up again after it hit troubled times in the early 1960s.

The 65 years since then have proved to be a period of great endeavour and, apart from the occasional blip, almost unbroken growth and success. Now with the next generation of Stannahs – Jonathan (Jon), Patrick, Alastair, Nicholas (Nick) and Helen – in the family business the future looks very bright, although they too face the usual business challenges of competition in the market-place and cost pressures.

There are many aspects of their family history of which the Stannah family can be proud, but perhaps two stand out. First, they have shown a determination through thick and thin to stick to their last, and second, they *make* things. We cannot argue with the success of the service industries in the UK today, but great countries are made by inventing, developing and manufacturing products.

Stannah has always made things and, most important, things that people want at a price they are prepared to pay. That is their great achievement and legacy.

'I HAVE TABS ON HIS GRANDFATHER'

Solomon Stannah was born on 10 July 1800 in Cheadle, Cheshire. Solomon's father, William, had married Ann Ash by special licence, since she was a minor. Harold Parkhouse, son of Mary Elizabeth Birtt, the daughter of Elizabeth Mary Stannah, herself the daughter of Solomon Stannah, helped Brian Stannah assiduously in the 1980s in tracing the Stannah family history. He wrote this in April 1982:

> I have found out who Solomon's father was, his date of birth and I think I have tabs on his grandfather!
>
> Enclosed is a copy of a rough lay out of our discoveries from which you will see that it is established that William did in fact marry twice, as you thought, – his first wife was ANN ASH whom he married by special licence as she was a minor on 18.6.1787 and you will see the revised list of children by her – including Samyntas – son of Samuel, grandson of William and Ann.
>
> William was born on 30.1.1763 but I don't know the date of his death.
>
> William was described as a husbandman, which is I think a small farmer but we have discovered that William's father was one Josiah Stannah who was described as a Yeoman. The yeomen of England … were really the backbone to England at that time – he lived near Cheadle at a place called Horton in Staffs and must have had

1.1 Solomon Stannah. Born in July 1800 and married to Elizabeth Bradford, the daughter of a glove-maker in Worcester in 1829, he was a deeply religious non-conformist. Solomon and Elizabeth settled in Worcester where he worked in a draper's shop.

some land as it is on record that he left a coppice to his son Thomas and an annuity of £15 [about £1,650 in today's money] to William and Ellen. He died in 1806 so he was probably born in the mid-1730s which gets us back over 270 years.

Solomon's mother died soon after he was born and William married Ellen Mills on 25 October 1802. Solomon, and his elder brother Samuel, were brought up by Ellen along with the four or five children she bore by William. Two of Solomon's step-brothers, John and Richard, emigrated to the USA. Richard's nephew, William R. Stannah, wrote this letter to Joseph Stannah (this must have been A.J. Stannah, grandson of Solomon) on 26 November 1918:

Ocean Beach
California
Nov 26th 1918

Joseph Stannah Esq.,
London, England

Dear Sir,

A few months ago in looking over the London Directory in Denver, Colorado, I was very much surprised at finding your name. Now I am very curious to know who you are – whether or not you are a son of Solomon Stannah. My uncle, Richard Mills Stannah left England about the year 1836. My father and his family came over in the fall of 1848, and I am the only son left of John Stannah's family, and now in my 78th year.

I was nearly three years in our Civil War, and in fairly good health. For many years I have had it on my mind to write to Birmingham to see what I could find out, but this is the first, and when it is convenient for you to take a look over the Doomsday Book to see if there is any property coming to me: and I am rejoicing as all Englishmen should over our great victory over the devilish Germans, but the cost in blood and treasure has been fearful.

Please reply to this soon as convenient as I may leave here in about two weeks, and I know that this will be a great surprise to you.

(signed) William R. Stannah
Ocean Beach, California,
North America

William owned a farm at Browedge near Cheadle, and Solomon was brought up there. He went to the USA with Samuel in 1816 but returned after a year, Samuel returning a year or so later. Both set a precedent later followed by Albert (A.J.) and Leslie (Pop). Samuel was obviously a very entrepreneurial type. This is what Harold Parkhouse, who as we have seen was the grandson of Elizabeth Mary Stannah and son of Mary Elizabeth Birtt and William Parkhouse, wrote to Brian Stannah in 1984:

… interesting – Samuel was our great grandfather's eldest brother (born 1794) so 6 years older than Solomon – he must have been the earliest Stannah entrepreneur as you will see from the document (see footnote) he intended to go on to Port

---

The document was a Certificate given by His Britannic Majesty's Consul for the State of Maryland dated 15th November 1817 at Baltimore referring to Samuel Stannah's intention to travel to Port au Prince on the island of Santo Domingo (presumably a reference to Hispaniola, of which Haiti (whose capital is Port au Prince) forms part.

au Prince in Santo Domingo. He must have gone to the States probably from Liverpool in 1816 (aged 22 years) – returning to England in probably 1818/19 as he married in 1820 and I imagine was then off to London – he was the one you remember who referred to a snug little distillery (I like that phrase) – and considered his brandy the best in London. His son was Samyntas definitely. I am beginning to wonder if there ever was an earlier one, cannot find any trace and it could be possible that the other painting is one of Samuel in his early days say around 1825/30?

'DO NOT FLING YOURSELF AWAY'

By 1826 Solomon was contemplating marriage and wrote to his brother, by this time in London, for advice on that and other matters. He was working in Cheadle in the linen and silk trade, and Samuel advised him to stay there as business in London, especially in the drapery trade, was not good. However, he did say that if Solomon was contemplating starting his own business, some experience in London might be useful. Samuel wrote:

BY ALL MEANS DO NOT FLING YOURSELF AWAY – a steady young man may always meet with chances to do well in marriage and BETTER HIS CIRCUMSTANCES.

1.2 Samuel Stannah. Born in 1794, he was Solomon's eldest brother. After a two-year visit to the USA as a young man, he returned and settled in London to become first a confectioner and then a distiller, specialising in brandy. In effect, he was the first modern Stannah entrepreneur.

Samuel would die at the relatively young age of 49 in 1843. On his death certificate his profession was given as Distiller, and the cause of death, Paralytic Apoplexy. This is what Harold Parkhouse wrote to Brian Stannah in the 1980s about Samuel:

I referred a little while ago to Lydia – Samuel's step sister who went evidently to stay in London with Samuel – she would have been about 18 or 19 I think – and of the commotion that she caused. Now I have often wondered what happened to Lydia after she reached London – whether she went on to Cheadle or whether she went on to see this chap who was so infatuated with her – that, of course, was the letter of 1826. The next letter of 1828 is also extremely interesting when Samuel wrote to Solomon asking if he could come down to London fairly quickly as he wanted to consult him about a Brandy distillery, as he thought the house next door would make a 'snug' little distillery. He evidently must have come down because one of the next things one knows about Samuel is that he got his distillery going. His confectionery business in Regent Street had evidently been very successful because he must have gone down to London, I think in 1821 and by 1826 and 1827 he was listed in the commercial directory for those two years as 'Samuel Stannah, Confectioner of 94, Regent Street, The Quadrant' so I think that in 1828 or 1829 he must have sold this or let it as there was some reference in one of those letters to a rent of £200 per year which would have been a lot, and he evidently got his distillery going. He didn't live over the business but lived in Princes Street, Lambeth and in 1838 (about nine years afterwards) he is in the directory as 'Samuel Stannah – Brandy Distiller of Princes Street'.

It is rather interesting about this Brandy distillery because where he got his recipe (or whatever one does with brandy distilling) I have no idea but evidently it was good brandy – I suppose he imported in bulk and did the distilling – I have never quite discovered how it was distilled but he said his brandy was the best in London and he was having great trouble with the customs. Anyway this must have been overcome as in 1842 he had taken on another partner, a Mr Sinclair, who had the 'Kings Arms' in Lambeth and they apparently went into business as a partnership. They were then trading under the name of Stannah, Sinclair and Company and I would imagine they were very successful but how they marketed their brandy I have no idea – I think it may have been supplied in bulk as I have never been able to discover if it was under a brand name, if that was sold in London or if it was sold all over the country – I rather think it must have been sold in bulk. The partnership, however, did not last very long as Samuel died in 1843 when he was 49.

I would not be too bold as to suggest that he died from too much of his own brandy – I would not think that was the case at all. So in a sense that was the end of an era and the beginning of another because it was in 1841 in the first national Census he was shown living in Princes Street with his wife Emma, Samyntas (son) and another son called Augustus – now this son Augustus I have never been able to trace – whether he died in earlier years I don't know but I have no idea what happened to him – perhaps he was in the business I don't know but evidently Samyntas

1.3 Samuel Stannah's death certificate. He died of Paralytic Apoplexy at the comparatively young age of 49 in 1843. Nothing to do with the brandy, of course.

who would have then been about 22 took charge of the business and it was renamed Samyntas Stannah & Co. Whether Mr Sinclair was still in the business then I don't know – there is no record. Evidently the business must have been large because they took in another business in Whites Road, Lambeth, another premises and in 1852 they moved to Little Moorfields which was in the City.

Samyntas is a very unusual name, I have never heard of it before, I can find no particular records of what happened to him – of course he married and had three children I think. His move to Little Moorfields was evidently very successful and the business quite clearly prospered. There are no particular records from 1852 onwards until he sold the business or transferred it (I have been unable to find any records of this) and he quite clearly retired in 1872 and he must have done very well and got himself well known and made quite a lot of money because he retired to 12 Gower Street London W and was then put down in the directory as 'Samyntas Stannah Gentleman' and he lived there until he died in 1874 at really quite an early age – only 53. His widow, Emma, when she died, left £48,384 [about £5 million in today's money]. In his will he left nearly everything to his wife Emma but there was one interesting bequest which I will refer to later of £500 to the Royal National Lifeboat Institution and he was evidently very keen on this.

Brian Stannah has commented that Pop 'always referred to a <u>gin</u> distillery and that Samuel's wealth remains in Chancery'.

The lifeboat *Samyntas Stannah*, provided out of a legacy from Emma Stannah to the RNLI (and named in accordance with the wishes of the testatrix), was launched in 1891 and remained on duty at the Orkney Station until 1904. She took to sea several times and was credited with saving 52 lives. A long poem appeared in the magazine *The Lifeboat* on 1 August 1899. Here are the first and last verses:

1.4 The lifeboat Samyntas Stannah *was launched in 1891,
remaining on duty at the Orkney Station until 1904.*

The Aith Hope Longhope Lifeboat Crew

To the Coxswain and Crew of the Aith Hope Lifeboat, *Samyntas Stannah*, I respect-fully dedicate these simple verses for their noble work on the night of 31 October 1898, in connection with the disabled steamer *Manchester City*, during a north-west gale in the Pentland Firth.

> They are no fancy regiment
> Of a spick and span brigade,
> They wear no brilliant uniform
> To march with on parade;
> No pipe or drum to cheer them on
> When siccar work to do;
> 'Tis the music of the tempest song
> Leads on the Lifeboat crew.
>
> Let us cheer the Aith Hope Lifeboat
> And all her noble band;

They have shed a brilliant lustre
Upon their native land.
In days when they and I are gone
'Twill be a household tale
How the men of Brims crossed Torness race
In that October gale.

R. Robertson
Master of the Orkney Mail steamer, *St Ola*
Daisybank, Stromness

On 16 July 1829, Solomon had married Elizabeth Bradford, the daughter of a glove-maker in Worcester. Solomon, a deeply religious non-conformist, kept a little black book and in it he wrote about his marriage and the births of all his children.

[We] were married after an intimate acquaintance of more than two years during which time we both experienced a great degree of warmth and mutual affection being influenced in all our proceedings by motives of the purest love and resorting continually to a throne of grace to seek that wisdom which was necessary to guide and direct in matters of such vital importance to our present and eternal happiness. In all the varied circumstances through which we had to pass only one sentiment seemed to prevail, a strong and anxious desire to commit this cause to Him who cannot err, and in laying the whole matter candidly before our Heavenly Father and waiting a proper time for the moving of that Divine Spirit without which nothing can be effectively accomplished we had the satisfaction of knowing that every subsequent event tended to strengthen and unite us in heart and mind and strongly to confirm our first opinion that an all wise and gracious providence had not been consulted in vain but was leading us in a right path making all things work together for our good in connection with His own glory. May grace mercy and truth dwell richly in each of our hearts. May it ever be our constant study to cultivate every Christian grace and to promote each other's temporal, spiritual and eternal welfare, mutually seeking by faith and prayer those covenant blessings which our God and Father hath made over to us and designed that we should feed upon as the bread and water of eternal life that we may be strengthened with almighty power energy and grace to go forward in our Christian cause triumphing over sin and the world and in all our yet unknown steps have to testify that the Lord our God is present to help and that He will never leave nor forsake those who confide in Him.

He ended with the words:

This God is our God for ever and for ever and He will be our guide even unto death and when heart and flesh fail He will be the strength of our hearts and our portion for ever.

Solomon moved to Worcester to work in a Mr Hill's draper's shop. Elizabeth struggled with almost every birth of her children. The first, a girl, delivered on 12 August 1830, was stillborn. The second, a boy, born in June 1831, lived for only a few months. The third, a boy, born in July 1832, lasted only 36 days. The fourth, another boy, born in July 1833, and named Richard Solomon, lived for three and a half years. The fifth, a girl, born in May 1835, was christened Elizabeth Mary. She lived to grow up, marry and eventually die at the age of 90. Along the way she had two children, Maude, who was born in 1870 and died at the age of 90 in 1960, without marrying, and Mary Elizabeth, who married William Parkhouse and had two children, Gladys and Harold. (Harold was in constant communication about the family history until his death in 1991.) Finally, on 1 November 1836, Joseph was born, and this is what Solomon wrote later:

> On November 1st 1836 a few minutes before 8 o'clock on Tuesday night Mrs Stannah was delivered of a very fine boy after a short but sharp struggle which she bore remarkable well, being better in health and stronger than on any former occasion. The child takes the breast the second day very quiet and good. He was baptized at Bradport Chapel by the Rev. E. Lake on Sunday, December 18th 1836 (Joseph). We were led to give him this name from a variety of concurring circumstances both before and after his birth. The admirable and interesting character of Joseph was the

1.5 Elizabeth Stannah. Like her husband Solomon, she was also born in 1800. After many difficult births and early deaths of several children, she eventually gave birth to a daughter who survived into adulthood, and a son, Joseph, who would found the Stannah family lift business.

frequent subject of conversation having just read over his history and being reminded of him frequently by a picture I purchased representing Joseph introducing his father Jacob to Pharaoh King of Egypt who had arrived at the zenith of his prosperity and power being the sole ruler and director of the affairs of all the Egyptian Empire. On this memorable occasion Jacob in answer to some questions put to him by Pharaoh among other things he informs him in his own peculiarly impressive manner that he is 130 years old so that Joseph at this time must be 41. Jacob lives 17 years after and dies in peace at the advanced age of 147, though he was distinguished by the clearest marks of divine approbation yet in general his was a life of suffering and trouble whereas his son Joseph with a few years' exception was a life of splendour and prosperity.

When Solomon died in 1875, this obituary appeared in the *Malvern News*:

THE LATE SOLOMAN STANNAH.

We very briefly announced in our issue last week, the death of Mr. Soloman Stannah, and now we add a few particulars concering him. He was taken ill in London, but died in Worcester. It seems he went to that city about the year 1826, and was engaged in the establishment of the late Mr. Geo. Hill, of the Cross, Mr. Joseph Fisher and Mr. W. Towndrow were there at the same time. After a few years he commenced business for himself in High-street, and subsequently opened a branch concern at Malvern, which he carried on successfully for some years, when he retired from business, and resided in one of his own houses (No. 1 Portland-place) till about eight years ago, when he returned to Worcester, taking up his abode in Rainbow Hill-terrace, where he lived greatly respected and beloved. Laying himself out doing good, his charity both public and private, were unostentatious and by no means inconsiderable. He has left behind him a son, an engineer, in London, and a daughter, married to the Rev. W. B. Birtt, the minister of the Countess of Huntingdon's Chapel, Lowesmoor, Worcester. His remains were interred in the Malvern Cemetery on Monday, in the grave containing those of his wife.

1.6 Solomon Stannah's obituary in the Malvern News.

In Affectionate Remembrance

OF

SOLOMON STANNAH,

OF WORCESTER, (LATE OF MALVERN),

BORN JULY 10th, 1800.

DIED MAY 5th, 1875.

AND WAS INTERRED IN THE CEMETERY, MALVERN, MAY 10th, 1875.

—o—

" I know in whom I have believed."

1.7 A card that was given to all Solomon Stannah's friends at his funeral.

JOINED AN ENGINEERING FIRM

Joseph lived with his mother Elizabeth, father Solomon and sister Elizabeth Mary, above the family business in Worcester High Street. In 1849, the family moved out to Malvern, a lovely village on the edge of the Malvern Hills and later home to two excellent public schools, one for boys, the other for girls. Solomon opened a branch of the business and bought three houses in Portland Terrace. The family lived in Number One. (Note the later family connection with Malvern described in Chapter Two.) By this time, Elizabeth Mary, or Lizzie as she was always known, was at a boarding school in Chester and in 1850 her mother wrote to her: 'Your dear brother is gone to school – so much had to be done to his teeth he could not go before – he is most anxious about you.'

1.8 Joseph Stannah. The son of Solomon and Elizabeth, Joseph is the founder of the Stannah family business. An inventive man, he took out a number of patents and by 1890 was able to boast of 'Gold Medals for Lifts and Cranes'.

Joseph became interested in engineering and was apprenticed to the Great Western Railway works in Wolverhampton. The 1850s was, of course, boom (and bust!) time on the railways. We know that Joseph worked there because he appeared in a concert at the Stafford Road Institute in Wolverhampton sponsored by Great Western. The programme for the evening shows Joseph singing 'Tears of Memory' in the first half and 'The Spell' in the second half. Joseph clearly possessed a good singing voice and would continue to sing in concerts and church services for the rest of his life. Later this was to be a talent also possessed by his grandson Leslie's wife, Jean, as described in Chapter Two.

It is interesting to see Joseph's background and training at the Great Western Railway works. Clearly this provided a sound foundation for a career in engineering, as a similar path was followed by W.O. Bentley, the founder of Bentley Motors Limited, and R.J. Mitchell, the Chief Designer for the Supermarine Aviation Works (later to become Vickers Supermarine Limited) with many famous designs to his credit, including the Schneider Trophy-winning S5, S6 and S6B seaplanes and, of course, the Supermarine Spitfire. The value of a training in practical engineering is beyond doubt and is still a feature of the Stannah company in the 21st century.

In the early 1860s Joseph went to London and joined an engineering firm in Southwark Bridge Road called W.H. Sisterson. He soon married Elizabeth Cuxon, whose family had been gold-beaters and gold and silver wire-drawers in the City

[COPY.]

GREAT WESTERN RAILWAY

Stafford Road Institution Soiree,

15th DECEMBER, 1859.

PROGRAMME OF THE ENTERTAINMENTS.

PART I.

INTRODUCTORY ADDRESS	... ...	Mr. ARMSTRONG.
GLEE	"Glorious Apollo."	Mr. STANNAH.
SONG	"Tears of Memory."	
ADDRESS	... ...	Mr. J. GILL.
WALTZ	... ...	STAFFORD ROAD BRASS BAND.
SONG	"Nelly Brallagan." ...	... Mr. J. NEWBY.
RECITATION	... ...	Master BECKETT.
PIANOFORTE SOLO ...	... "Fantasia."	... Miss A. WHITE.
SONG	"Far, Far, upon the Sea." ...	Mr. RICHARDS.
SONG	... "Bonnie Dundee." ...	Master BARNETT.
	... ...	STAFFORD ROAD BRASS BAND.
SONG	"The Holy."	... Mr. WHITE.
CONCERTINA	"Dream of Love,' —Waltzes. ...	Mr. T. CLAYTON
SONG	... "The Country Gaby." ...	Mr. J. WORRALL.
ETHIOPIAN ENTERTAINMENT ...	Messrs. STANNAH, BULL, WRIGHT, DEAN, BAIRD, & PAINTER.	

AN INTERVAL OF EN MINUTES.

PART II.

Exhibition of Magic Lantern, and Descriptions	... ...	Mr. BARNETT.
GLEE	"Dame Durden." ...	...
FLUTINA	"Do not Mingle."	Mr. T. CLAYTON.
RECITATION	... ...	... Master E. RILEY.
SONG	"The Railway."	Mr. WRIGHT.
ADDRESS	... ...	Mr. WHITE.
SONG	... "The Spell	...Mr. STANNAH.
PIANOFORTE SOLO ...	"Still so gently."—Somnambula. ...	Miss A. WHITE.
SONG	"Come whoam to thy Children and me." ...	Mr. PILKINGTON.
ADDRESS	... ...	... Mr. DEAN.
SONG	"Good Bye, Sweetheart, Good Bye." ...	... Mr. WHITE.
	"Silver Lake,"—Varsoviana.	STAFFORD ROAD BRASS BAND.
SONG	"To the West." ...	... Mr. W. ROBERTS.
GLEE	"Ye Gentlemen of England." ...	
CONCLUSION	THE NATIONAL ANTHEM.	

1.9 Joseph was apprenticed to the Great Western Railway works in Wolverhampton. Here he is performing in a concert sponsored by Great Western. He was in good company, as both Henry Royce and W.O. Bentley spent apprenticeships on the railways – in their case, the Great Northern Railway.

of London for a number of generations. Previous Cuxons had been Freemen of the City of London as far back as 1722.

After their marriage, Joseph and Elizabeth lived at 55 Bridge Street, Southwark and had four children: Albert Joseph, the eldest, born 6 August 1868, May, Amy and Louise.

In 1867, the business, W.H. Sisterson, was reconstructed and Joseph must have taken control, for in 1877 this appeared in the commercial diary:

> Stannah Joseph (late W.H. Sisterson) GENERAL ENGINEER and Patent Crane Maker for wine cellars, improved lifts and cranes for warehouses, hotels, hospitals by STEAM and HAND power.

By this time the address was 18–20 Southwark Bridge Road London S.E.

In 1867 Joseph's sister, Elizabeth Mary, married the Reverend William Bridges Birtt and lived in Worcester, where William was minister at a church in the town. In 1875 the Reverend was raising money to clear off a debt on the church and Joseph Stannah contributed no less than £200 (about £22,000 in today's money).

As mentioned above, it seems almost certain that Joseph Stannah set up his lift and crane manufacturing business in Southwark in south-east London in the 1860s. However, advertisements for J. Stannah lifts in the late 19th century have 'Established 1828' printed on them. This might refer to the founding of Sisterson, although the first mention in the *Post Office London Directory* is in 1838 when Sisterson, Walter, Engineer, 1 Morris Place, Southwark Bridge Road appears. See also the advertisement in *The Builder* of 13 January 1877 which, *inter alia*, says: 'J STANNAH, late W H SISTERSON and ESTABLISHED 1835.' A bit of a mystery here.

SOUTHWARK

Southwark received its name from the 'south work' of a river wall to match its northern counterpart. The whole area of Southwark is covered with Roman burial sites. It was an important meeting point during the Roman occupation as travellers began their journey south, and it was also the starting point of the Canterbury pilgrimage told by Chaucer. The church of St Mary Overie, later St Saviour, later Southwark cathedral, became a sanctuary for those fleeing justice in London and, as a result, by the 17th century there were no fewer than seven prisons in the area, the most famous being the Clink (giving rise, of course, to the phrase: 'He's in the clink.'). Oddly, although the area was owned by various religious authorities, including the Archbishop of Canterbury, it was also known for its licentiousness. The prostitutes of Bankside, carrying on their trade within the 'Liberty' of the Bishop of Winchester, were known as 'Winchester Geese'.

The development of south London grew apace after the building of Westminster Bridge in 1750 and Blackfriars Bridge nineteen years later. New highways led south

1.10 An early sewing machine of the 1860s. Technology was being spread far and wide as the industrial revolution gathered pace.

from the bridges, opening up Kennington and the Elephant and Castle. As Peter Ackroyd pointed out in his *London, The Biography*:

> The new roads led to fresh industrial development, so that the vinegar- and dye-works were complemented by potteries, lime kilns and blacking factories. By 1800, Lambeth had assumed all the characteristics of a slum. Yet the area still grew … The process acquired restless momentum in the first decade of the nineteenth century when three toll bridges were completed. Southwark Bridge, Waterloo Bridge and Vauxhall Bridge opened the way for the extensive building programmes which created south London in its present form.

Initially Joseph Stannah worked on cranes, goods lifts and hoists from tiny premises in Southwark, but the company was involved in the early stages of the development of passenger lifts or 'moving rooms' as they were known. The company's early publicity included the slogan: 'A passenger lift is never put in action except it has to raise or lower HUMAN BEINGS and therefore must be safe beyond DOUBT.'

Early lifts were quite different from those seen today, and in London they were often hydraulically powered, moving silently between floors. Lift cars were elaborately finished with wood and metal work, typical of the Victorian and Edwardian eras.

In the middle of the 19th century, department stores were expanding and competed with each other to provide their customers with the latest amenities such as plate glass windows, cash-registers, pneumatic tubes for orders and payments, and lifts. Wylie and Lochhead, the department store in Glasgow, installed the first lift in 1855. The *Glasgow Herald* described it as:

... a very ingenious hoisting apparatus worked by a neat steam engine, which is intended not only to lift up bales from the Wagon entrance to the upper parts of the building, but to elevate those ladies and gentlemen to the galleries to whom the climbing of successive stairs might be attended with fatigue and annoyance. Parties who are old, fat, feeble, short-winded, or simply lazy, or who desire a bit of fun, have only to place themselves on an enclosed platform or flooring when they are elevated by a gentle and pleasing process to a height exceeding that of a country steeple.

An interesting insight into the history of Stannah arose when Kay West, who worked in the Stairlifts factory and whose hobby was collecting antiquarian books, bought from an Andover bookstall a copy of *The Quarterly Review*, Vol. XLVI, November 1831 and January 1832, published by John Murray in 1832, which was found to have as part of its binding an advertisement for Stannah Lifts dated 4 August but annoyingly with the year trimmed off. However, the advertisement was from a magazine called *Engineering* which was not published until 1866. This suggested, or actually proved, that the binding was a rebinding. Jocelyn Sharpe, on behalf of Brian Stannah, carried out some research in 2005. This was the result taken from her note to Brian:

I had a nice call from Michael Pattinson, the chap at the British Library regarding the letter I sent him regarding the old Stannah advert in *Engineering*.

He said he had the idea of looking up on a Victorian calendar in which years the date of Aug 4th fell on a Friday (the day of publication of *Engineering*) and there were two dates – 1876 and 1882.

Engineering was first published in 1866. However, the first copy that is held by them is from 1871 (several previous copies are missing). The bad news is that having got hold of the early copies to have a look on our behalf, unfortunately there are no front pages, or contents – or adverts.

Michael says that he thinks that whoever actually bound these copies together for records purposes must have taken these parts of the magazines out – possibly the adverts were in the back as a separate section – probably thinking this would save space and that the adverts wouldn't be needed in the future.

Your friend had previously said that the typeface used was probably around 1860.

He then talked with a colleague regarding the actual Patent itself – and managed to find out that the date that the 'Stannah Pendulum Pump' patent was applied for was 24th April 1876. He, therefore, thinks that the date of the old advert is likely to have more likely been around the 1882 date. (Also he says in the copies 'August' became abbreviated to just 'Aug' around that time.)

It might be interesting to see here how far the lift industry had developed by this stage. Mark Doble wrote this in *Elevation* in 1994 (*Elevation* is the very successful Stannah in-house magazine 'For the staff, by the staff', published annually since 1985):

1.11 The Grand Hotel in Trafalgar Square. Built in the 1870s, this was a typical example of the taller buildings being erected in London in the second half of the 19th century, providing potential contracts for Stannah's lifts.

The history of the lift industry goes back some 150 years, and today in this country two names stand out – Otis and Stannah.

Elisha Otis is regarded as the father of the modern lift, and Stannah are the world leaders for stairlifts.

But where did it all begin?

Elisha Otis launched his safety lift at the New York Exhibition in 1853. This incorporated a rack which ran the full height of the lift shaft. In the event of a rope breaking, springs forced bars into notches on the rack, preventing the lift car from dropping. Otis demonstrated this system personally at the Exhibition by standing in a suspended lift car while the ropes were cut away with the cry of 'All safe, Gentlemen, all safe'. An amazed and enlightened audience saw the successful birth of the modern safety lift.

But the story actually begins much earlier than all this. In fact it rightly begins back in 1743 in France. Louis XV had a lift built for his exclusive use at the Palais de Versailles. The lift was attached to the outside of the building, unlike most lifts today which are situated inside. This lift car was counterbalanced and driven from an overhead winding gear and motive power supplied by hand. But scant regard was paid to safety in those early days.

Back to the nineteenth century: in 1857 Otis installed the first steam driven elevator serving four floors in a top New York store.

By 1889, Otis had developed another historical first, the electric elevator. Unwittingly he also gave birth to the skyscraper, by giving rapid access to all levels of buildings with several storeys. Previous prejudices against such structures became obsolete virtually overnight.

Early lifts had been hauled by hemp rope or chains, but steel wire rope was soon realised to be a much more durable and effective alternative. Traction design dominated the early passenger lift market for over 80 years. But the last 20 years has seen a shift to hydraulic lift technology (which was common in the very early days) which is more versatile, enabling the motor room to be sited anywhere and not necessarily attached to the lift shaft. There is now no need for roof-top motor rooms with hydraulic power, and thus building lines can be smoother.

The word 'hydraulic' is derived from the Greek *hydro* meaning water and *aulos* meaning a pipe.

By the 1880s buildings were being designed with the elevator in mind. The construction of the Eiffel Tower in 1889 incorporated various lifts at the design stage. Still one of the tallest structures in existence today, the first stage of the tower was originally reached by a Combaluzier lift driven by two powerful hydraulic engines. This lift car could carry an incredible 100 passengers. The second stage could be reached by the Edoux elevator. This was the only vertical lift on the structure as the others had to deal with the angled legs of the Tower. The water for the hydraulic lifts was pumped 1,000 feet to the top of the Tower and stored in a massive tank.

The Eiffel Tower lifts were eventually replaced by electric traction lifts, but by then they had given many years of reliable service.

1.12 The Foreign Office in Whitehall. Large government offices were also potential customers.

1.13 An advertisement (or cartoon?) depicting a German stairlift in 1893, provided by Stannah's current distributor in Germany, Lifta.

Around the turn of the century (1900) the growing demand for power in some cities was satisfied, not only by gas and electricity, but by pressurised water mains able to drive machinery. In London, the London Hydraulic Power Company installed their system under the streets, into which building owners and companies could tap, providing an energy source alternative to electricity with rams and pistons used in place of motors.

Many early lifts were operated by hydraulic rams or 'jiggers'. These were sometimes positioned in the roofs of buildings and, by means of a multi-part roping system around the ends of the hydraulic ram, the lift was caused to rise and fall in the lift shaft in response to expansion or contraction of the ram, with power derived from these high-pressure water mains. Later these were superseded by electric motor-driven traction lifts, followed by the swing back to hydraulic lifts that Mark Doble has described. In the 1990s, the pendulum began to swing back towards traction lifts again, although not without strong competition from the Stannah Lifts range of hydraulic passenger lifts. More of this continuing story is told in later chapters. As we move into the 21st century, the situation is evenly balanced in the low- to medium-rise passenger lift sector between the hydraulic systems and compact traction arrangements, Stannah taking a leading position with their products being developed to offer both options.

In other words, *Plus ça change, plus c'est la même chose.*

J. STANNAH,

Late W. H. SISTERSON,

ENGINEER,

20, SOUTHWARK BRIDGE ROAD,

LONDON, S.E.

STEAM or HAND CRANES,

For Wharfs, Warehouses, Factories, &c.

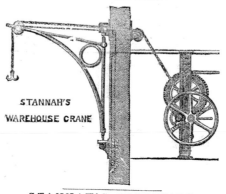

STANNAH'S

WAREHOUSE CRANE

STANNAH'S "SPECIAL"
DINNER LIFT,
With Break, for Mansions, Club Houses, Hotels, &c.

SINGLE

OR

DOUBLE

LIFTS,

BY STEAM

OR

HAND POWER.

BASEMENT

AND

INCLINE LIFTS.

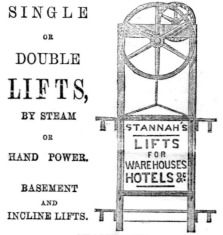

STANNAH'S
LIFTS
FOR
WAREHOUSES
HOTELS &c.

STANNAH'S

PATENT SAFETY APPARATUS.

To Prevent the Box or Cage Falling, in the event of the Main Rope or Chain Breaking.

Should be applied to all Lifts used for raising Passengers or valuable Goods.

It is applicable to Lifts with Wood or Iron Guides.

ESTABLISHED 1835.

1.14 An advertisement placed by Stannah in The Builder *in January 1877. Note the claim 'ESTABLISHED 1835'. (Other advertisements claimed 1828.)*

STANNAH PATENTS

Both Joseph and A.J. Stannah were inventive men who made many patent applications, some of which succeeded in being granted patent protection. These included:

1875   Safety apparatus for lifts or hoists
1876   Donkey engines and pumps
1877   Pendulum pump
1878   Arrangement and working of slide valves for steam engines, pumps and other purposes
1878   Improvements in stuffing boxes or glands applicable to the piston and slide rods of steam, air and water cylinders and other like purposes
1888   Improvements in hydraulic hoisting machinery
1889   Variable power hydraulic apparatus
1901   Improvements in or connected with glands

The company continued to make patent applications into the 21st century.

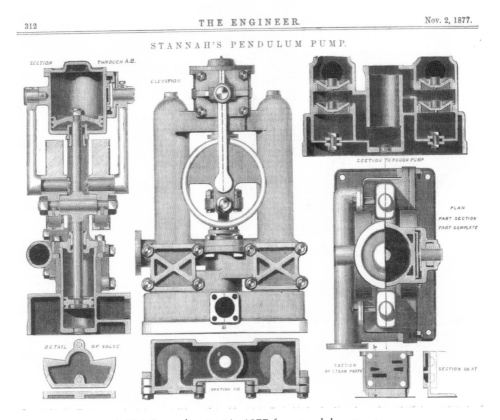

1.15 A Stannah patent in 1877 for a pendulum pump.

MAY 24, 1889.   THE ENGINEER.

VARIABLE POWER HYDRAULIC APPARATUS.

MR. J. STANNAH, SOUTHWARK BRIDGE-ROAD, ENGINEER.

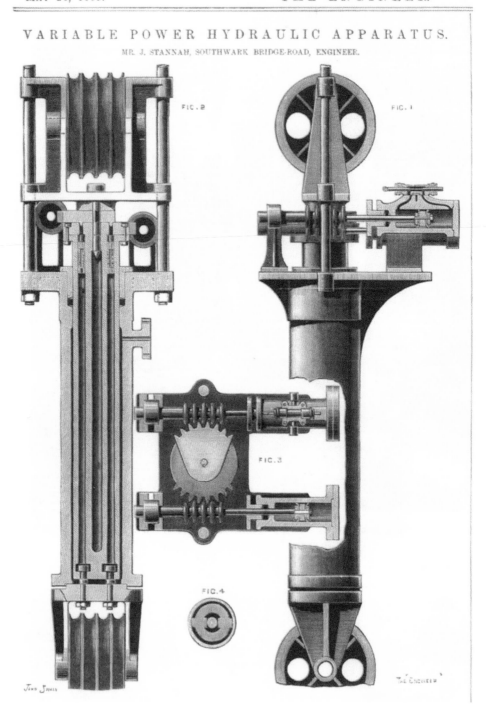

1.16 A Stannah patent in 1889 for variable power hydraulic apparatus.

An advertisement appeared in *The Times* of 30 July 1877 offering premises fitted with Stannah cranes:

> To be Let, in the heart of the City (Paternoster Square, formerly Newgate-market), new, strongly built, and very handsome WAREHOUSES and OFFICES, specially suitable for carpet, linen, and woollen trades, printers, publishers, and others requiring light, space and great facilities for unloading goods in a central position. Among the conveniences of these buildings is an entrance for carts and wagons from Warwick Lane. The warehouses are fitted with Stannah's cranes. Rents moderate. Apply to Mr James Beal, 20, Regent Street, S.W.: or on the premises.

In the 10 July 1880 copy of *The Builder – A Journal for the Architect, Engineer and Operative*, various suppliers of building components were listed in what could correspond to our present-day classified ads. Among the products advertised were 'Guaranteed, safe and noiseless gas, hydraulic, steam and handpower lifts' by Arch. Smith & Stevens; Bunnett's Patent Lifts; 'Gas, hydraulic and handpower lifts and cranes' by R. Waygood; 'Lifts, hoists and cranes – specializing in the hotel and restaurant trade' by F. Goddard; 'Steam and gas engines, hoists, cranes and lifts' by Henry J. Coles; 'Hydraulic, steam, gas and handpower lifts for hotels, hospitals and asylums' by G. Waller & Company, and 'J. Stannah, Engineer's, four types of lifts – hydraulic, gas, steam and handpower.'

The Times of 16 March 1910 carried this announcement:

> ELECTRIC LIFT CONTRACT – The contract for electric lifts at Messrs. Richard Clay and Sons' new printing works, now being built in Southwark, has been given to Mr. J. Stannah. Five lifts, all with push button control, are to be provided – four goods lifts to deal with loads of one ton at a speed of 80ft. per minute, and a passenger lift to deal with a load of 7½ cwt. at 120ft. per minute. The driving will be on the V sheave principle, the sheaves being driven by means of worm geared electric motors. The lifts are being made in accordance with the specifications of Mr Frank Broadbent, the consulting engineer to Messrs. Richard Clay.

The advertisements on the following pages show that Stannah was already established as a brand name for safe and reliable lifts.

1.17–1.21 (overleaf) Advertisements for the Stannah range. When advertising their lifts, Stannah said: 'All lifts listed in these sheets have been designed with the same careful attention to detail. Where one lift is rendered simpler and cheaper than another, this result is always attained by the omission of certain features – never by cheapening of any part of the lift equipment.'

510

Hand Rope Control.

ELECTRIC PASSENGER LIFT. 5 Persons at 120 feet per minute.

Lift No. 1.

Fig. 1.—Controller.

Fig. 2.—Car.

Fig. 3.—Winding Gear.

J. STANNAH, Skin Market Place, Bankside,

Telegrams :
"Lifts Boroh London." **LONDON, S.E.**

Telephone No. 1365
Hop.

26

511

Car Switch Control.

ELECTRIC PASSENGER LIFT.   5 Persons at 150 feet per minute.

Lift No. 2.

Fig. 4.—Cage.

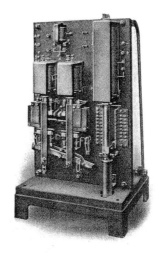

Fig. 5.—Controller.

Fig. 6.— Winding Gear.

J. STANNAH, Skin Market Place, Bankside,

Telegrams :
"Lifts Boroh London."   **LONDON, S.E.**

Telephone No. 1365
Hcp.

27

512

Car Switch Control.

ELECTRIC PASSENGER LIFT.   6 Persons at 175 feet per minute.

Lift No. 3.

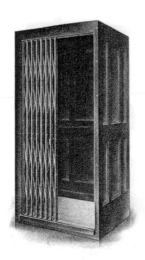

Fig. 7.—Cage.

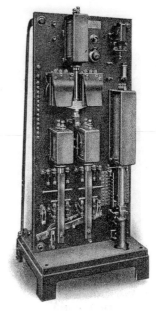

Fig. 8. Controller.

Fig. 9.—Winding Gear.

J. STANNAH, Skin Market Place, Bankside,
Telegrams: **LONDON, S.E.**   Telephone No. 1365
"Lifts Boroh London."   Hop.

Car Switch Control.

ELECTRIC PASSENGER LIFT.

8 Persons at 200 feet per minute, or with 2 speed control 250 feet.

Lift No. 4.

Fig. 10.—Cage.

Fig. 11. Controller.

Fig. 12.—Winding Gear.

Fig. 13.—Car Switch.

J. STANNAH, Skin Market Place, Bankside,
LONDON, S.E.

Telegrams :
"Lifts Boroh London."

Telephone No. 1365
Hop.

514

Automatic Control by Push Buttons

ELECTRIC PASSENGER LIFT.   5 Persons at $\frac{100}{125}$ feet per minute.

Lift No. 6.

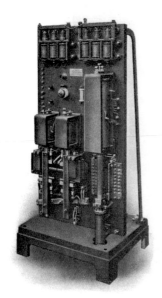

Fig. 14.—Controller.   Fig. 15.—Cage.   Fig. 16.—Push Panel.

Fig. 17.—Winding Gear.

J. STANNAH, Skin Market Place, Bankside,

Telegrams :
" Lifts Boroh London."   **LONDON, S.E.**   Telephone No. 1365
Hop.

GOLD MEDALS FOR LIFTS AND CRANES

The Times in 1881 regularly carried advertisements for cranes, lifts, Patent Pendulum Donkey Pumps at £4 10s (about £495 in today's money), and a Southwark high-speed 26hp engine for £15 (£1,650), all to be supplied by J. Stannah, 20 Southwark Bridge Road.

Boom followed by slump has happened fairly regularly in the British economy in the 20th century and, in the 21st, was repeated in 2008. It happened also in the 19th century, and Joseph Stannah would have had to cope with it in the 1860s. Britain's general economic progress was interrupted by two financial crises. The Companies Act of 1862 was followed by a rush of company flotations but, as with all such bubbles, the bad were floated with the good, and in 1866 one of the City's major banks, Overend Gurney, collapsed, taking down with it some others including the General Credit and Finance Company of London, a financial institution set up to meet the needs of growing manufacturing companies. Ten years later, a trade depression brought down the West of England and South Wales District Bank and the City of Glasgow Bank. The City of Glasgow Bank turned to the Bank of England and asked it to supply cash against the security of the loans made to Glasgow shipbuilders, but the Bank of England, run as a private bank by City merchants and bankers, did not feel itself under any public obligation and was not inclined to help.

By contrast, in 2007 when one of the English banks, Northern Rock, came under severe pressure and the television screens were filled with images of people queuing outside Northern Rock branches waiting to withdraw their money, the Bank of England stepped in to rescue the bank and it was eventually nationalised by the Labour government.

Further crises occurred in the 1880s. As Sir Robert Ensor wrote in *England 1870–1914*:

> The second crisis started in 1882 in Paris; where the collapse through over-speculation of a great banking house (the Union Générale) paralleled closely the panic of 1866 in London. But it was succeeded in 1883 by a continued fall in prices, which lasted three years and at its climax in 1886 produced ... serious rioting in London and elsewhere. This slump of the eighties, following so soon after that of the seventies and linked to it by the unlifted depression in agriculture, gave Victorian courage and optimism the severest shock that it had yet received. Among its by-products were a Lord Mayor's Fund (memorably maladministered); a circular from the local Government Board to the local authorities urging relief works; a royal commission 'on the Depression in Trade and Industry', which buried itself under the pile of its own blue-books; and a hot stirring of social thought ... Soon after Lord Salisbury's second government got into its stride, the sky cleared; and before the end of 1887 trade was working towards another boom.

Through all these troubles Joseph Stannah survived, and on 28 July 1890 J. Stannah, Engineer, based at 20 Southwark Bridge Road, London and boasting 'Gold Medals for Lifts and Cranes', tendered for a hydraulic lift to Messrs Wiggans (*sic*, should be Wiggins), Teape, Carter & Barlow at 10 Aldgate London EC:

1.22 A tender offer for the paper supplier, Wiggins Teape, in July 1890. Note the 'GOLD MEDAL for LIFTS and CRANES'.

1.23 A letter following up the original tender offer.

The 10 cwt Suspended Hydraulic Goods Lift with iron-framed cage 4'6" × 3'0" × 5'0" high, iron guides for a rise of 47'6" with joint plates and fixing brackets, overhead chain sheaves on turned pins, with bearers and uprights, Hydraulic hoisting machinery of improved construction with turned ram, ram guides and sheaves to multiply 8 to 1, with improved lubricators, cylinder, gland, stuffing box, best hydraulic packing, operating valve with gun metal and phosphor bronze fittings, hand rope passing up through cage with automatic checks at top and bottom of journey, stop and back pressure valve, supply and fix all necessary piping inside the building, cut and trim openings in floors, and leave all in working order for the sum of ninety nine pounds [about £11,000 in today's money]. Patent Safety Apparatus extra … £18 [£2,000]. This is exclusive of any alterations or repairs, should any be required, they would be extra.

Delivery and erection of the lift was included in the £99. Terms of payment were: first 75 per cent on completion and the balance 'in one month'.

The tender concluded:

Your order will be much esteemed
Yours faithfully
J Stannah

We have ended this chapter in 1900, although this is a somewhat arbitrary choice as the date of the transition of responsibility for running the company from Joseph to his son Albert is not known, but it would have been around this time. Albert had already been to the USA where, *inter alia*, he had done some teaching in New York and had been highly praised for it by the Superintendent of Schools.

It was also at this time that Joseph Stannah either moved his business from 20 Southwark Bridge Road to nearby Skin Market Place, Bankside, or added these premises to the first. Certainly, *Kelly's Post Office London Directory* carried this entry in 1899:

Stannah, Joseph – LIFTING APPARATUS MAKERS, hydraulic & hand lifts & cranes; Southwark – lift gears in nearly 50 sizes – 20 Southwark Bridge Road S E.

Whereas in 1901 the entry was:

Stannah, Joseph, engineer – Hydraulic passenger lifts, goods lifts & cranes, by hand, steam, gas or hydraulic; patent balance lifts & variable power hydraulic cranes, in connection with the Hydraulic Power Company's mains: donkey and other team pumps, hydraulic pressure pumps, presses, intensifiers & fittings, dinner lifts and lift gears etc. – Skin Market Place, Bankside S E.

The illustrations of Joseph's products show that he had a well-developed product range that must have been market-leading at that time. The control panels, winding gears and other equipment shown in the advertisements give us an insight into the technical capabilities of the company that Joseph had developed over the 30 years since he had adopted control.

As the company moved into the 20th century it had reached a peak in the scale of its operations, with the maximum level of output of 58 machines being delivered in 1897. As well as building a thriving business, Joseph Stannah found time to lay down a few thoughts on how to lead a happy life and, at the same time, a successful business (see illustration 1.24).

It would take another two generations of Stannahs, two world wars and 50 years before such a scale of production was to be reached again.

1.24 (opposite) Some 'Rules of Life' as commended by Joseph Stannah. It was a kind of Ten Commandments for running a happy life and creating a successful business.

SOME RULES OF LIFE

1. HAVE A PLAN LAID BEFORE-HAND FOR EVERYDAY

2. ACQUIRE A HABIT OF UNTIRING INDUSTRY

3. CULTIVATE PERSEVERANCE

4. CULTIVATE THE HABIT OF PUNCTUALITY

5. BE AN EARLY RISER

6. BE IN THE HABIT OF LEARNING SOMETHING FROM EVERY MAN WHOM YOU MEET

7. FORM FIXED PRINCIPLES ON WHICH TO THINK & ACT

8. BE SIMPLE & NEAT IN YOUR PERSONAL HABITS

9. ACQUIRE THE HABIT OF DOING EVERYTHING WELL

10. MAKE CONSTANT EFFORTS TO BE MASTER OF YOUR TEMPER

11. CULTIVATE SOUNDNESS OF JUDGMENT

12. OBSERVE A PROPER TREATMENT OF PARENTS, FRIENDS & COMPANIONS

Found amongst the papers of the late
Joseph Stannah esq. of Bankside London S.E.

Superintendent of Schools,

Yonkers, N. Y. Mar. 27, 1894.

To whom it may concern;
Mr. A. J. Stannah has taught mechanical drawing in our evening
school the past winter and has been
very successful in the work. He
had two classes under his exclusive
control and direction. His instruction
was admirably directed to the whole
class as well as to the individuals,
and the progress during the winter
was marked. In my experience of
many years I have not had a
teacher of this branch superior to
Mr. Stannah. If he were to remain
here he would be asked to continue
his work in our evening schools
in years to come. I wish to add
an expression of my pleasure in
all my intercourse with him.
He is in every respect an earnest,
honorable gentleman.
Yours truly,
Charles E. Gorton.

1.25 Albert Stannah went to the USA, where he did some teaching
of mechanical drawing, and received this glowing endorsement from
the Superintendent of Schools in Yonkers, New Jersey in 1894.

CHAPTER TWO

1901–1945

'The lamps are going out all over Europe'

ALREADY COMPETITIVE

Advertisements in *The Builder* in 1904 show that there was plenty of competition in the lift industry. Alongside a simple one for 'J. STANNAH – Lifts, Cranes' were ones for:

1. Archd. Smith & Stevens of Queen's Road, Battersea offering LIFTS. Safety Silence. ELECTRIC and HYDRAULIC 'RELIANCE' For Passenger Goods. Lifts of all other types.
2. CLARK, BUNNETT & CO. Ltd. LIFTS, CRANES, IRON DOORS. Original patentees of revolving shutters. New Cross Road SE and 22, Queen Street E.C.
3. WAYGOOD LIFTS. Falmouth Road, SE.
4. S HASKINS & BROS. 20, 22 and 24 OLD ST. EC. LIFTS – Fixed, complete.
5. Moffatt & Eastmead Ltd. Green Street, Blackfriars SE. SELF-SUSTAINING LIFTS, BELTPOWER, HANDPOWER, HYDRAULIC, ELECTRIC.
6. OTIS ELEVATORS. 4, QUEEN VICTORIA STREET, E.C.

7. RICHMOND'S LIFTS. 30 Kirby Street, E.C.
8. PICKERINGS Ltd. Globe Elevator Works. STOCKTON-ON-TEES LIFTS. Electric, Gas, Steam, Hydraulic, Hand-Power.
9. SPRAGUE 'SIMPLEX' ELECTRIC ELEVATORS. 48 in use on Central London Railway. METROPOLITAN ENGINEERING ASSOCIATION, 4 QUEEN VICTORIA STREET, LONDON E.C.
10. ALDOUS & CAMPBELL. BELVEDERE BUILDINGS, SOUTHWARK S.E. LIFTS and CRANES of all types manufactured.

2.1 *Advertisements in* The Builder, *February 1904, highlighting the competition that Stannah faced.*

The founders of Aldous & Campbell, Aldous and Campbell themselves and two others called Halliday and Long, had all worked for Joseph Stannah. (This was revealed by William (Bill) Sturgeon in the US publication *Elevator World*, when he visited the UK in 1982.) Of those companies listed above, in addition to Stannah, only two are still in existence independently. Otis, itself a subsidiary of United Technologies Inc. in the USA (which also owns the aero engine manufacturer, Pratt & Whitney), is said to be the largest lift manufacturer in the world, and Pickerings is another long-established family business like Stannah.

A ROLLER-COASTER RIDE

Fortunately, records were kept by J. Stannah of cranes and lifts, including their specifications from 1884 to 1928. The entries for 1884 are:

HYDRAULIC MACHINERY

1884 – 2 machines	Crane Lift	Dia.	Stroke	Purchase	Travel	Weight of Cylinder	Load Revised
1487 Powell, London Bridge	12cwt	6½"	7'0"	1 to 8	56 ft	24.0.0	14cwt
1492 Page Draper, Weston Street	5cwt	4½"	6'11"	1 to 8	53 ft	15.2.14	

Five machines were supplied in 1885 and another five in 1886, one to Westminster Hospital. A big jump to ten machines supplied took place in 1887, three to Glyn Mills bank, and another big jump to 27 in 1888, three to Phoenix Wharf. 1889 was not so good with only fifteen, one to the Salvation Army, but there was a recovery in 1890 to 24. 1891 brought 33 but 1892 brought a slump to ten. Recovery in 1893 brought 23, followed by 25 in 1894, 32 in 1895, 42 in 1896, 58 in 1897, 40 in 1898, 48 in 1899, 46 in 1900, 28 in 1901, and 27 in 1902. (The Boer War had an adverse effect on confidence in the British economy.) Recovery came in 1903 with 53 machines supplied, of which two were low-pressure lifts, two were pedestal cranes, six were suspended lifts, five suspended draw rod lifts, eleven were cranes and fifteen direct acting lifts. 1904 saw deliveries of only 24 machines and 1905 only eighteen, 1906 21, 1907 28, 1908 21, 1909 25, 1910 nineteen, 1911 thirteen, 1912 fifteen, 1913 only eight and 1914 only eight again.

The First World War broke out in August 1914 and there are no records of any lifts or cranes being delivered in 1915 or 1916. In 1917 there are records of two deliveries, nothing in 1918, and then five in the first year of peace, 1919.

Meanwhile, records show that from 1902 to 1928 these were the deliveries of electric lifts and cranes:

1902	Two
1904	Six

1905	Five
1906	Seven
1907	Three
1908	Three
1909	Ten
1910	Seventeen, of which three were passenger lifts and fourteen goods lifts
1911	Five
1912	Ten – four passenger and six goods
1913	Eleven
1914	Six
1915	NIL
1916	NIL
1917	One
1918	NIL
1919	One
1925	One
1926	One
1927	One
1928	Three

Whereas the deliveries of hydraulic machinery had been almost exclusively to London addresses, a number of the electric lifts and cranes went to customers further afield. For example, there were deliveries to Cape Town and Johannesburg in 1908 and 1909 and to Huddersfield in Yorkshire in 1912.

In the leaner of the above years, one can only assume that other engineering activities supported by repairs and service kept the business afloat.

AN EARNEST AND HONOURABLE GENTLEMAN

On 1 July 1896 Albert Joseph Stannah married Edith Coltman at the Abney Chapel, Church Street, Stoke Newington in the District of Hackney in the County of London. He was 28 years old, described as a bachelor whose profession was Mechanical Engineer and whose father was Joseph Stannah, also a Mechanical Engineer. His wife Edith was 22 years old, was given no profession, and her father, William Coltman, was described as a Licensed Victualler. His address was given as Ashcroft, 1 Elmfield Road, Bromley, Kent and hers as Rosslyn, 115 Brooke Road, Stoke Newington.

A.J. Stannah did not confine himself to the manufacture of lifts. A history of the village of Boreham in Essex published in 1988 says that in 1911 a Mr Joseph Stannah (it must have been A.J. because Joseph Stannah, as we are calling A.J.'s father, died in 1907), described as an 'Electrical Engineer' of Old Hall, Boreham (more recently used by the Ford Motor Company as a training centre), built a small factory locally known as 'the Nuts and Bolts Works'. Apparently there were six

2.2, 2.3 Albert Stannah also built a small factory in the village of Boreham in Essex. During the First World War a row of houses was built behind the works (reputedly by German prisoners of war). These houses were known as Stannah cottages. The assumption was that the Stannah works was engaged on war production.

dwellings on Brick House Lane, which Boreham provided for his workmen. It also says in the history that the factory in Boreham manufactured lifts, and continues:

By late 1916 it had been dismantled and transferred to North London where it still trades under the name of Stannah Stairlifts. [This was not quite correct, as the move was to Southwark, south of the Thames, and the correct Group identity is Stannah Lifts, which incorporates Stannah Stairlifts.]

*2.4 A crowd in Berlin cheering the outbreak of war on 4 August 1914
(note that Adolf Hitler was in the crowd).*

2.5 In reality, not much to cheer about.
Thirty per cent of British men aged between 20 and 24 died in the conflict.

2.6 Harry Russell, Brian and Alan's maternal uncle,
served in the Seaforth Highlanders during the First World War.

A.J. Stannah kept a notebook which ranged over many subjects, showing that he possessed what could best be described as 'an enquiring mind'. At one point he is defining static induction, the next electric circuits, and then he moves on to Ohm's Law. He follows this with an instruction manual on soldering. Next we have 'Selected Dates 1918–30', and those selected show that his main concerns were with the state of peace and war, the government and the economic situation. None of these interests is surprising for a man engaged in business in those difficult years.

The 'diary' begins with:

1918   Nov. 11 Armistice

Static Induction -

When an electrified conductor is brought near another conductor which has not been electrified, an electric charge will be INDUCED in the latter

ELECTRO-STATIC FIELD

The range of space over which the electrified plate A has the power of inducing a charge in B is called the ELECTRO-STATIC FIELD

DI-ELECTRIC

The strength of the induced charge depends on the distance between the conductors: it also depends on the medium (non-conducting) between the two bodies. The non-conducting medium (such as air) is called a DIELECTRIC.

Static Induction is the principle underlying the construction of a Condenser.-

Condensers - CAPACITY.

Static induction is the principle underlying the construction of condensers. The property a condenser has of holding a large or small charge of Elect. is called its CAPACITY

The CAPACITY of a condenser depends on 3 factors (1) The area of the plate: (2) The thinness of the dielectric. (3) The inductive capacity of the dielectric

(NB.) The facility with which a dielectric allows static induction to act is called its INDUCTIVE CAPACITY. If the space between plates is filled with glass a stronger charge will be induced than if the space is filled with air.

ELECTRIC CURRENT.

An electric current is a flow of Elect.
To flow there must be a difference of electric pressure or POTENTIAL
This difference of POTENTIAL is called E.M.F.

2.7 A page from A.J. Stannah's notebook showing his 'enquiring mind'.

1919 notes:

Feb 27	Industrial Conference, London (General Conference of Employers' and Workmen's Associations: recommended 48 hour week and minimum wage)
Mar 3	Sankey Coal Commission
June 28	Peace Treaty signed at Versailles
July 16 to Aug 15	Yorkshire Coal Strike
Sept 22 to Jan 22	Iron moulders' Strike
Sept 25 to Oct 5	Railway Strike
Oct 29	International Labour Conference, Washington (Recommended universal regulation of hours of work on the basis of 48 hour week)

1920

Aug 9	Unemployment Insurance Act
Sept 24	International Financial Conference – Brussels
Oct 18 to Nov 4	Coal Strike
Nov 15	First Assembly of the League of Nations

1921

June 11	Irish Peace Conference
Apr 11 to July 1	Coal Strike
June 6 to 24	Cotton Strike
June 19	British Population Census
Aug 31	OFFICIAL TERMINATION OF WAR
Nov 6	Anglo-Irish Treaty signed

1922

Jan 6 to 13	Conference of Allied Powers – Cannes
Jan 16	Irish Free State formally into being
Mar 12 to June 13	Engineering Strike
Mar 29 to May 6	Shipyard Strike
Apr 1 to Aug 15	USA Coal Strike
April	Genoa Conference of Powers (Considered the means of restoring European trade especially with Russia. Former enemy powers represented)
Nov 15	CONSERVATIVE GOVERNMENT

1923

Jan to Dec	Coal Strike in Ruhr District
Jan 8	French occupied Ruhr
Feb 1	Anglo-American debt terms settled
Apr 1	Irish Free State excluded from UK in Trade Returns

Apr 13 to Nov 24	Strike of Boilermakers in Shipyards
Nov 24	German Mark stabilised at 4,200,000,000,000 marks to $1

1924

Jan 22	LABOUR GOVERNMENT
Apr 9	Dawes Reparations Report
July 17 to Aug 22	Building Strike
Aug 16	London Conference – Dawes Scheme accepted
Oct 29	CONSERVATIVE GOVERNMENT

1925

May 1	British return to Gold Standard
July 31	Government subsidy to Coal
Sept	Samuel Coal Commission appointed
Oct 16	Locarno Conference Agreement (Peace and security pacts in Europe leading to Germany's admission to the League of Nations)

1926

May 1 to Dec 1	Coal Strike
May 4 to 12	GENERAL STRIKE
Aug 23	German Mark open to free exchange
Sept 8	Germany admitted to League of Nations

1927

May 4	World Economic Conference at Geneva
Aug 22	Argentina returned to Gold Standard
Oct 12	Poland returned to Gold Standard
Dec 22	Italy returned to Gold Standard

1928

May 1	Norway returned to Gold Standard
May 14	Greek currency stabilised
June 14	French currency stabilised
Aug 27	Kellogg Peace Pact signed
Nov 22	Treasury Note Issue taken over by Bank of England
Dec	Distress in mining areas

1929

Jan to May	Reparations Conference in Paris
June 5	LABOUR GOVERNMENT
Aug 31	Hague Conference (settled dates of evacuation of Rhineland)
Sept	Crisis in New York stock market

2.8 The Stannah workforce at Skin Market Place, Bankside, probably at the end of the First World War.

It might seem strange now that A.J. Stannah seemed *so* obsessed with industrial strife but we should remember how many revolutions and overthrows of governments had taken, and were still taking, place around the world. Many of the upper and middle class of Britain were in a state of apprehension about the stability of the country. The excellent social historian, Arthur Marwick, wrote in his *Britain in Our Century*:

The Twenties
Working-Class Militancy and Economic Depression

Twenty, or even ten years ago much of the historical discussion over the first postwar decade centred on the question 'why was there no revolution in Britain?' Even today much energy and subtlety is still being expended on this question. Marxist writers, who are foremost in believing that a revolution ought to have taken place, have stressed both the long-term quiescence of the British working class and such short-term factors as the national solidarity fostered by war, as well as the skilful policies of Britain's governments. Recently an American scholar, James Cronin, one of the leading proponents of that form of social history which, in the tradition of the continental sociologists, concentrates on the shifting relationships and conflicts between different economic interest groups, has stated the argument that there was a special 'crisis' in Britain in 1919–20 which, but for the skilful containment policies of the government, might have had issue in revolution.

Marwick's chapter includes photographs of trade unionist Willie Gallacher lying unconscious on a Glasgow street after being hit by a police truncheon, tanks on the streets of Liverpool during the town's police strike in 1919, and armoured cars at Hyde Park Corner during the General Strike of 1926.

Nevertheless, it was not all bad news. A.J. Stannah might have lightened the tone of his diary entries by noting that in 1930, 2,218,000 motor vehicle licences were issued (this was more than double the 952,000 of 1922); then there was the establishment of the British Broadcasting Corporation in 1926 and the transmission of the first television picture by John Logie Baird, also in 1926.

After this diary A.J. Stannah returned to what seems to have been his first love – electricity – with three very detailed pages of notes and drawings on early telegraphy. And then these are followed by three pages of detailed descriptions and drawings of Tinman's Tools.

In the piece which the American, William Sturgeon, editor of the US journal, *Elevator World*, wrote about Stannah during his visit in 1982, he said: 'A.J. Stannah continued to operate the business when times were very difficult in the depression following the First World War.'

A.J. Stannah, along with almost every other businessman in Britain, and indeed the world, had to cope with a horrendous worldwide depression. This depression of the early 1930s was precipitated, if not fully caused by, the Wall Street Crash of 1929. The US economy had expanded very rapidly in the 1920s but the pace was such that it could not last, and the wisest realised it when President Hoover assured his countrymen in 1928: 'We are nearer today to the ideal of the abolition of poverty and fear … than ever before in any land.'

For people in the USA *were* making money, and not just businessmen. Business did boom but, as is often the case, the stock market boomed more, and almost everyone was in on the act. (This is not quite true. There were about 1 million investors, but they made enough noise both before and after the crash that it seemed like almost everyone.) What made the explosion in prices possible was the trading 'on margin'. People were buying stocks and putting up only a tenth of the money. It was the obvious and easy way to get rich. You have or can scrape together $1,000. Normally this won't buy you much on the market, but if you can buy $10,000-worth of stock and that stock doubles, you have turned your $1,000 into $11,000. And plenty of people did. Others didn't stop to contemplate what might happen if the stock didn't double or if the totally impossible happened – it fell in price. When that happened, you had committed yourself to pay $10,000 and your stock is worth $7,000, no sorry, that was yesterday, today it's $6,000. And it got worse. A leading steel stock, surely the safest investment around, fell from $90 to $12. Within a month, shares fell by a third; they paused and even rose slightly in April 1930 ('a dead cat bounce'), before plunging again for the following two years so that, by the middle of 1932, the average industrial share was 15 per cent of its 1929 level. The effect on real America was traumatic and no one, except the very poor who had nothing to lose, escaped. (A few very rich, very canny people did, of course. Rockefeller is supposed to have walked into his office a week before the crash, when stocks were still going through the roof, and said to his chief clerk: 'Sell everything we have.' 'But sir,' protested his clerk. 'Listen,' said Rockefeller, 'I've just heard two boot-blacks discussing stocks. Who's going to buy from them? Sell!') Samuel Insull, who donated the Opera House to Chicago, heard the mutterings of the starving in the soup queue outside it, and increased his bodyguard from two to 30.

IN THE LIFT BUSINESS, BUT NOT IN THE STANNAH LIFT BUSINESS

Leslie Noel Stannah was born in 1901, the first son of Albert and Edith. He did not work in his father's business but was sent to the United States in the 1920s where he worked for the Haughton Elevator Company in Toledo, Ohio. (His father, A.J., had been to the USA in the 1890s where, among other things, he did some teaching of mechanical drawing at a school in Yonkers, New Jersey.)

2.9 A.J. Stannah, his wife Edith, and sons Leslie (standing) and Colin in 1921.

2.10 Leslie Stannah (third from right) leaving for the USA in 1922.
Young Colin is in front of him, A.J. on his right and Edith on his left.

Leslie's interests as a young man had centred around motorcycling. He was retained as a 'works rider' by Ariel, who were pleased to see him 'on the podium' at the end of many events. There are records of his winning cups and medals in motorcycling long-distance endurance trials. In 1924 Leslie was presented with silver cups for winning the Edinburgh and District Motor Club Scottish Trials and the North West London Motor Club London to Gloucester Trials. He also won many medals, including a silver medal in the London Motor Cycling Club London to Exeter Endurance Trial on 26 and 27 December 1921, another silver medal in the London to Lands End trial on 14 and 15 April 1922, another silver medal in the Reigate and Redhill District Motor Cycle Club Night Trial on 27 May 1922, a gold medal in the London Motor Cycling Club trial from London to Exeter on 26 and 27 December 1923, a bronze medal in the Surbiton Motor Club Melland Cup Trial on 8 March 1924, a gold medal in the Motor Cycling Club London to Edinburgh Trial on 6 and 7 June 1924, and a silver medal in the Ealing and District Motor Cycling Club rally from London to Holyhead in 1924.

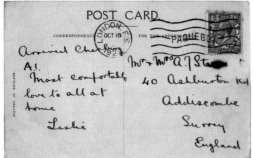

2.11–2.15 Postcards from Leslie Stannah to his mother and father from the SS Aquitania as he sailed to the USA, and to brother Colin, wishing him a happy birthday from Toledo, Ohio.

2.16 Leslie Stannah on one of his beloved motorcycles.

2.17 Leslie competing in the Scottish Six Days Trial in 1924 on his Ariel motorcycle.

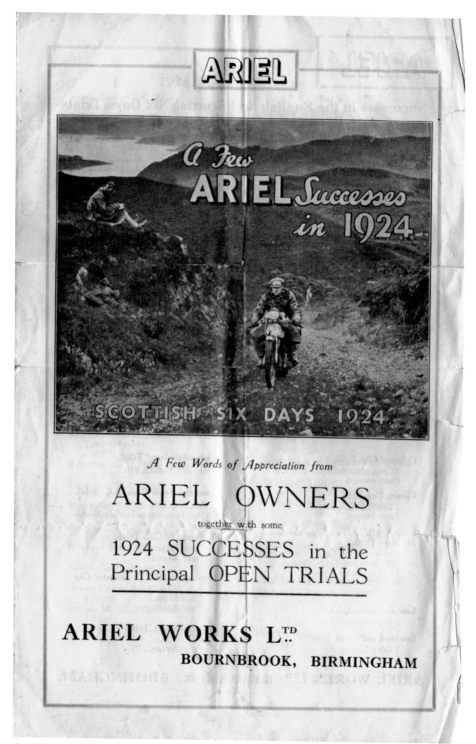

2.18 It was such a good photograph that the manufacturer used it in their advertisements.

*2.19 Leslie on another motorcycle endurance trial,
this time from London to John O'Groats.*

He returned to England from the USA after about eight months in the autumn of 1922 and worked first for A. and P. Stevens in Glasgow and then as Branch Manager for the Manchester lift company, Etchells, Congdon and Muir, subsequently acquired by Hammond and Champness of Walthamstow, where Alan Stannah, his younger son, later served his apprenticeship. However, he was not completely cut off from his family home in Addiscombe near Croydon in Surrey, and on 15 October 1927 he married his near-neighbour and tennis club girlfriend, Jean Russell.

Jean, like Leslie's grandfather Joseph, had a fine singing voice. Her music teacher wrote after a competition: 'As far as I can judge, you sang your item as nearly perfectly as I can ever hope or expect; the voice was clear and smooth, the "tone colour" varied and beautiful, and the rendering ideal.' Jean, accompanied by her pianist older sister Clara, travelled around south London to take part in competitions and recitals. Had she wished, she could have made this her career, but she chose instead to support Leslie and her family.

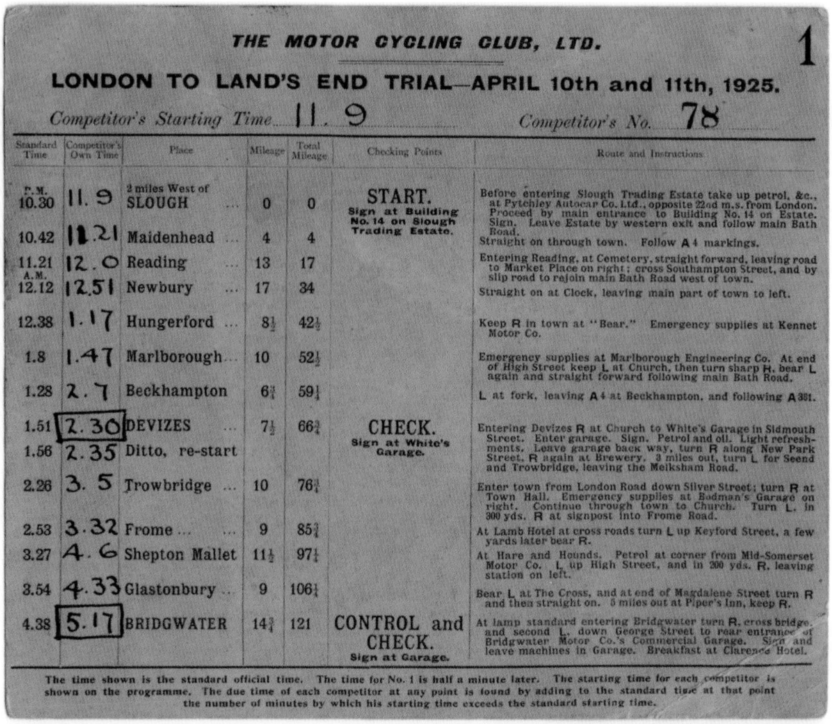

THE MOTOR CYCLING CLUB, LTD. 1

LONDON TO LAND'S END TRIAL—APRIL 10th and 11th, 1925.

Competitor's Starting Time 11. 9 *Competitor's No.* 78

Standard Time	Competitor's Own Time	Place	Mileage	Total Mileage	Checking Points	Route and Instructions
P.M. 10.30	11. 9	2 miles West of SLOUGH	0	0	START. Sign at Building No. 14 on Slough Trading Estate.	Before entering Slough Trading Estate take up petrol, &c., at Pytchley Autocar Co. Ltd., opposite 22nd m.s. from London. Proceed by main entrance to Building No. 14 on Estate. Sign. Leave Estate by western exit and follow main Bath Road.
10.42	11.21	Maidenhead	4	4		Straight on through town. Follow A 4 markings.
11.21	12. 0	Reading	13	17		Entering Reading, at Cemetery, straight forward, leaving road to Market Place on right; cross Southampton Street, and by slip road to rejoin main Bath Road west of town.
A.M. 12.12	12.51	Newbury	17	34		Straight on at Clock, leaving main part of town to left.
12.38	1.17	Hungerford	8½	42½		Keep R in town at "Bear." Emergency supplies at Kennet Motor Co.
1.8	1.47	Marlborough	10	52½		Emergency supplies at Marlborough Engineering Co. At end of High Street keep L at Church, then turn sharp R, bear L again and straight forward following main Bath Road.
1.28	2. 7	Beckhampton	6¾	59¼		L at fork, leaving A 4 at Beckhampton, and following A 361.
1.51	2.30	DEVIZES	7½	66¾	CHECK. Sign at White's Garage.	Entering Devizes R at Church to White's Garage in Sidmouth Street. Enter garage. Sign. Petrol and oil. Light refreshments. Leave garage back way, turn R along New Park Street, R again at Brewery. 3 miles out, turn L for Seend and Trowbridge, leaving the Melksham Road.
1.56	2.35	Ditto, re-start				
2.26	3. 5	Trowbridge	10	76¾		Enter town from London Road down Silver Street; turn R at Town Hall. Emergency supplies at Bodman's Garage on right. Continue through town to Church. Turn L. In 300 yds. R at signpost into Frome Road.
2.53	3.32	Frome	9	85¾		At Lamb Hotel at cross roads turn L up Keyford Street, a few yards later bear R.
3.27	4. 6	Shepton Mallet	11½	97¼		At Hare and Hounds. Petrol at corner from Mid-Somerset Motor Co. L up High Street, and in 200 yds. R, leaving station on left.
3.54	4.33	Glastonbury	9	106¼		Bear L at The Cross, and at end of Magdalene Street turn R and then straight on. 5 miles out at Piper's Inn, keep R.
4.38	5.17	BRIDGWATER	14¾	121	CONTROL and CHECK. Sign at Garage.	At lamp standard entering Bridgwater turn R, cross bridge, and second L, down George Street to rear entrance of Bridgwater Motor Co.'s Commercial Garage. Sign and leave machines in Garage. Breakfast at Clarence Hotel.

The time shown is the standard official time. The time for No. 1 is half a minute later. The starting time for each competitor is shown on the programme. The due time of each competitor at any point is found by adding to the standard time at that point the number of minutes by which his starting time exceeds the standard starting time.

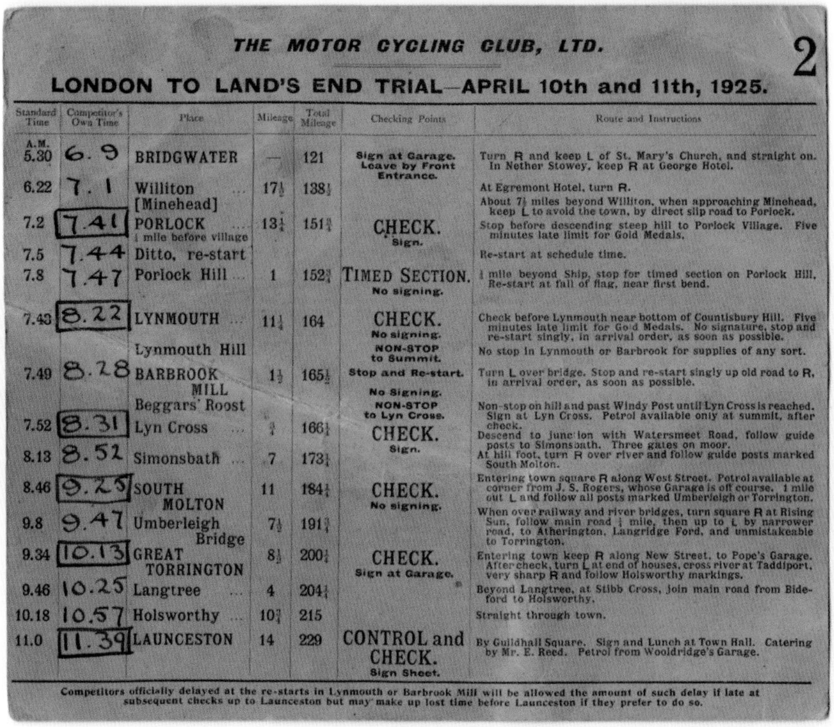

THE MOTOR CYCLING CLUB, LTD. 2

LONDON TO LAND'S END TRIAL—APRIL 10th and 11th, 1925.

Standard Time	Competitor's Own Time	Place	Mileage	Total Mileage	Checking Points	Route and Instructions
A.M. 5.30	6. 9	BRIDGWATER	—	121	Sign at Garage. Leave by Front Entrance.	Turn R and keep L of St. Mary's Church, and straight on. In Nether Stowey, keep R at George Hotel.
6.22	7. 1	Williton [Minehead]	17½	138½		At Egremont Hotel, turn R. About 7½ miles beyond Williton, when approaching Minehead, keep L to avoid the town, by direct slip road to Porlock.
7.2	7.41	PORLOCK ½ mile before village	13¼	151¾	CHECK. Sign.	Stop before descending steep hill to Porlock Village. Five minutes late limit for Gold Medals.
7.5	7.44	Ditto, re-start				Re-start at schedule time.
7.8	7.47	Porlock Hill	1	152¾	TIMED SECTION. No signing.	½ mile beyond Ship, stop for timed section on Porlock Hill. Re-start at fall of flag, near first bend.
7.43	8.22	LYNMOUTH	11¼	164	CHECK. No signing.	Check before Lynmouth near bottom of Countisbury Hill. Five minutes late limit for Gold Medals. No signature, stop and re-start singly, in arrival order, as soon as possible.
		Lynmouth Hill			NON-STOP to Summit.	No stop in Lynmouth or Barbrook for supplies of any sort.
7.49	8.28	BARBROOK MILL	1½	165½	Stop and Re-start. No Signing.	Turn L over bridge. Stop and re-start singly up old road to R, in arrival order, as soon as possible.
		Beggars' Roost			NON-STOP to Lyn Cross.	Non-stop on hill and past Windy Post until Lyn Cross is reached. Sign at Lyn Cross. Petrol available only at summit, after check.
7.52	8.31	Lyn Cross	¾	166¼	CHECK. Sign.	Descend to junction with Watersmeet Road, follow guide posts to Simonsbath. Three gates on moor.
8.13	8.52	Simonsbath	7	173¼		At hill foot, turn R over river and follow guide posts marked South Molton.
8.46	9.25	SOUTH MOLTON	11	184¼	CHECK. No signing.	Entering town square R along West Street. Petrol available at corner from J. S. Rogers, whose Garage is off course. 1 mile out L and follow all posts marked Umberleigh or Torrington.
9.8	9.47	Umberleigh Bridge	7½	191¾		When over railway and river bridges, turn square R at Rising Sun, follow main road ¼ mile, then up to L by narrower road, to Atherington, Langridge Ford, and unmistakeable to Torrington.
9.34	10.13	GREAT TORRINGTON	8½	200¼	CHECK. Sign at Garage.	Entering town keep R along New Street, to Pope's Garage. After check, turn L at end of houses, cross river at Taddiport, very sharp R and follow Holsworthy markings.
9.46	10.25	Langtree	4	204¼		Beyond Langtree, at Stibb Cross, join main road from Bideford to Holsworthy.
10.18	10.57	Holsworthy	10¾	215		Straight through town.
11.0	11.39	LAUNCESTON	14	229	CONTROL and CHECK. Sign Sheet.	By Guildhall Square. Sign and Lunch at Town Hall. Catering by Mr. E. Reed. Petrol from Wooldridge's Garage.

Competitors officially delayed at the re-starts in Lynmouth or Barbrook Mill will be allowed the amount of such delay if late at subsequent checks up to Launceston but may make up lost time before Launceston if they prefer to do so.

2.20, 2.21 The times that Leslie kept on the two-day trial in 1925.

2.22 Leslie and Jean on their wedding day, 15 October 1927.

Jean was very proud of her final report on leaving school and kept a copy of this throughout her life. (Report from R.J. Done, BA, Head Master and Principal: 'A pupil satisfactory in every respect, classwork, homework and conduct. She has taken a very active part in the social activities of the school, being the possessor of a beautiful singing voice and is very highly thought of not only by her school fellows, but by myself, and the rest of the staff'.)

Leslie still did not join the family business of J. Stannah run by his father, Albert. Instead, he left Etchells and joined Penrose Lifts (later acquired by Express Lifts) in the mid-1930s, serving as a Director until the outbreak of the Second World War in September 1939.

2.23 Leslie with new-born son, Brian, and grandma Edith in 1936.

2.24 Leslie and Jean with Brian on his birthday bicycle in 1938.

2.25 The Stannah family in the garden at West Wickham on Brian's birthday, 5 August 1938. L to R: Leslie, A.J. holding Brian, Edith and Jean. Sitting in front is A.J. and Edith's nanny/housekeeper, Daisy.

Leslie Stannah, as indeed did many others, anticipated the possibility of war and had already joined the Royal Naval Volunteer Supplementary Reserve (RNVSR). Furthermore, conscious of the potential danger of German bombing in the south of England, he drove his Wolseley Hornet with his expectant wife, Jean, and son Brian, born in 1935, non-stop from West Wickham in Kent to relatives of Jean in Bridge of Allan in Scotland. (Alan was born there in October 1939.) Leslie immediately then drove back to Addiscombe in Surrey and jacked up the Wolseley on bricks in Jean's father's garage for the duration of the war. He then left for HMS *King Alfred*, the newly opened training centre for RNVR officers. An extract from the Royal Navy Research Archive informs us that Pop must have been one of this first batch.

With the outbreak of the Second World War on September 3rd 1939, the Admiralty implemented its contingency plan training new officers to man the rapid expansion of the peace-time fleet. The plan called for the opening of a dedicated training establishment for Royal Naval Volunteer Reserve Officers at one of the eight RNVR divisional centres in the U.K. The Sussex Division, based in Hove, was chosen.

2.26 Leslie, having anticipated the outbreak of war in 1939, had joined the Royal Naval Volunteer Supplementary Reserve, and is seen here instructing young sailors.

The Hove Marina complex was to have been Hove's new municipal Swimming Baths and recreation Complex, due to be partially open to the public by September 1939. Instead the Marina opened its doors for the first time as a commissioned ship in the Royal Navy, becoming HMS 'King Alfred' on September 11th under the command of Captain John Noel Pelly CBE, RN (Ret).

King Alfred was the ninth century King of Wessex and he is considered to be the 'father' of the British Navy as the first monarch to utilise ships in defence of the realm. The new establishment which bore his name was to 'father' a new kind of naval officer to swell the ranks of Britain's soon to be rapidly expanding navy. These were HO (Hostilities Only) officers commissioned into the RNVR as temporary appointments; they were to be released from service on the cessation of hostilities. By the end of WW2 RNVR officers accounted for over 80% of the officers on active service with the Royal Navy.

Training was to commence at Hove almost immediately, the first batch of trainees was due to arrive one week later. Captain Pelly and his small staff set about organising the Marina's facilities into a training school, preparing a syllabus and to find suitable billets for staff and trainees in short order.

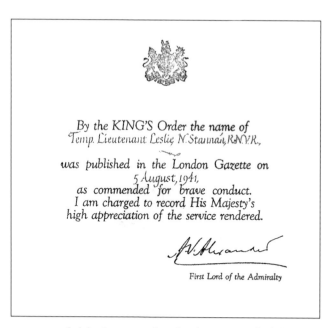

By the KING'S Order the name of
Temp. Lieutenant Leslie N. Stannan, RNVR,

was published in the London Gazette on
5 August, 1941,
as commended for brave conduct.
I am charged to record His Majesty's
high appreciation of the service rendered.

First Lord of the Admiralty

2.27 Leslie was commended for brave conduct by the First Lord of the Admiralty in 1941.

Leslie's letter to Jean at this time shows how couples had to face up to the heartache and uncertainties of separation, and their struggles to make some small provision should the worst befall.

2.28 A letter from Leslie Stannah from New Barracks at Gosport to his wife, Jean, whom he calls 'Kiddie', telling her how much he loves her and how he has provided for her and 'our two darling boys' in case the worst happens.

The Royal Navy archive goes on:

The initial batch of 140 men reported to King Alfred in late September 1939, a mixture of Supplementary reservists and direct entry recruits. The Royal Naval Volunteer (Supplementary) Reserve was a force of 2,000 yachtsmen and other experienced amateur or retired professional seamen over the age of 25 established in 1936 as a ready reserve of suitable men to become naval officers in times of emergency. The majority of the RNV(S)R were mature, experienced sailors who were fast tracked through 'King Alfred' and had an average stay of 10 days before they were granted commissions. For less experienced members of the RNV(S)R the standard training period was three months.

Leslie Stannah would have been one of the former.

2.29, 2.30 Leslie and
Jean with Brian and Alan
in 1940, and Jean with
Brian and Alan in 1941.

Alan Stannah, who as we've seen was born in 1939, has the following recollections of this time:

In order to be closer to Pop, and to avoid the dangers from bombing raids, for a time our mother Jean took us from our home in West Wickham, Kent, to stay in a number of guest houses, farms and rented accommodation. At The Brown Owl, Cold Waltham, near Pulborough, the introduction of two young children must have upset the routine of the elderly residents.

Living in Sussex took Jean and the boys away from the London area and its repeated bombing and closer to Lieutenant Leslie Stannah, now based at Portsmouth, where on the 5th August 1941 he was commended by the King as shown for brave conduct during enemy raids, which was accordingly published in *The London Gazette*.

Things were easier after a move to an adjacent village, Watersfield, where Peta's Cottage, Sandy Lane, provided a tranquil retreat, although signs of the war were ever present in wrecked planes in the nearby fields. A dispersal scheme for aircraft production took this into unlikely areas and in this quiet country lane we used to gather up spilt aluminium rivets that were being produced in a nearby cottage industry.

Then we later moved to three farms near Malvern and Ledbury to be close to Pop during his time at the shore training establishment, HMS *Duke*, at Malvern. Electricity was still to reach this area and I recall the farmer's wife using real iron 'irons', which were heated on the kitchen range with slip-on shiny bases after each re-heating. There was no central heating then, so in winter the inside of the windows was iced in beautiful patterns of frost (a delight that is unknown to most modern children) and our toothbrushes were often frozen in the washbasins.

There was no doubt about the dangers to Londoners and other city dwellers, as this memory of Brian Stannah makes clear:

The Anderson air raid shelter in our maternal Grandfather's garden at 43 Glenthorne Avenue, Addiscombe, Croydon, was a semi-subterranean concrete structure into which, during the Battle of Britain, Grandpa and Grandma Russell, Mother and her two sisters, our Aunts, Clara and Elizabeth, and Alan and I would all squeeze into an area as I recall of not more than six feet square. Dark and dank, but somewhat safer than being indoors. (For some reason we were living there temporarily.)

2.31 (opposite, top) An Anderson shelter, which was half-buried in the ground with earth heaped on top. They were made from corrugated iron sheets bolted together at the top and with steel plates at either end. The entrance was protected by a steel shield and an earthen blast wall. They measured only six feet six inches by four feet six inches internally and were dark and damp. People were reluctant to use them, especially at night, a time of course when they were most needed. By September 1939, the month war was declared, about 1.5 million had been erected in gardens.

2.32 (opposite, bottom) Morrison Shelters (named after the Minister for Home Security, Herbert Morrison) were introduced in March 1941 for use by people without gardens. The shelter, made of heavy-duty steel, could also be used as a table.

*2.33–2.36 Late in the war there was a renewed threat from the air for the London area:
the V-1 and V-2 missiles*

Later, in 1944, a Morrison indoor shelter was erected in the 'front room' at our parents' home at 116 The Grove, West Wickham. Named after Herbert Morrison [Herbert Morrison was a significant Labour MP who served in Winston Churchill's wartime Coalition government, first as Minister of Supply and then as Home Secretary], this shelter was made in steel like a table tennis table with angle iron legs, sheet steel top and wire mesh sides. This was where mother, Alan and I took refuge nightly when the German V1 rockets (known as 'doodle bugs') started to rain down on Southern England. I recall hearing them approaching overhead. That was fine. What we dreaded was the cessation of sound. That was when the rocket ran out of fuel. There would then be a period of silence, followed by the explosion as it came to earth, not targeting but indiscriminately decimating wherever it landed. One night the effect of the by now familiar drone, silence and bang too close for comfort in the morning revealed a pile of rubble a hundred yards or so down the road. Amazingly the Jackson family protected by their Morrison shelter survived.

Whilst aerial attacks were a nightly activity, as boys we scoured the nearby roads in the morning searching for the evidence, mainly in the form of shrapnel and occasionally, if lucky, finding a 'nose cone' maybe 40mm in diameter. When not at Greenhayes Prep School, I enjoyed helping the milklady (milkmen were now in the Forces). Taking the bottles to doorsteps and returning with the empties, then climbing back on to the cart. Yes, t'was horsedrawn and now and again we'd give the old nag a nosebag of feed and customers were ever ready with their hand shovels to collect the output from the previous feed for their gardens.

Alan, although only four in 1944, recalls the 'doodle bugs':

The sound of an enemy air raid warning siren in a film still makes my flesh creep 65 years later. Mother had made Brian and me 'siren suits' in a sort of grey blanket material similar to that worn by Winston Churchill, for cold nights in the shelter. When the alarm sounded, she first took Brian down to the shelter, then me, by which time Brian had gone back upstairs to bed. It must have been hard for her coping alone with two young boys under the nightly threat from the V1 and V2 missiles. I remember one warning which caused us to leave our breakfast porridge on the table. When we returned, the bomb blast had brought down the ceiling into my porridge. I remember crunching broken glass under our feet as we later walked down the road past the shattered houses.

In his book *The Second World War*, John Keegan explains the development of both the V-I, a flying bomb, and the V-2, a pilotless rocket:

The Germany army's decision to invest in a rocket development was motivated by the provisions of the Versailles treaty, which forbade it to possess heavy artillery but did not proscribe rockets … In October 1942 a successful test firing was staged, in December Speer, the Armaments Minister, authorised mass production, and on 7 July

1943, after viewing a film of a missile launch, designated it 'the decisive weapon of the war' and announced that 'whatever labour and materials [Braun and Dornberger, the two key scientists] used must be supplied instantly' ... On 12 June 1944 the first flying-bomb landed in Britain, 8 September was the first successful V-2 rocket attack. By then the Luftwaffe's 155 Regiment had been driven back from the positions whence its V-1s could reach England; as a result out of the 35,000 produced, only 9,000 were fired against England and of these over 4,000 were destroyed by anti-aircraft fire or fighter attack. The V-2s were never fired from their chosen launch sites in northern France; from Holland they could just reach London, on which 1,300 impacted ...

The V-2s killed 2,500 Londoners between 8 September 1944 and 29 March 1945.

Keegan does not say how many were killed by the V-1s. The answer was 6,184, nearly all in London. Their effectiveness had been countered by the early autumn of 1944. They did not fly faster than a Spitfire, and by September 80 per cent of them were being brought down either by fighter aircraft or anti-aircraft fire.

Leslie Stannah served throughout the war, attaining the rank of Lieutenant Commander and Divisional Commanding Officer of HMS *Duke*, the shore-based training establishment in Malvern, renewing the earlier family connection with this town. Meanwhile, during the war, A.J. Stannah's business had ceased trading, its premises having been destroyed by German bombing. In terms of the manufacture of lifts it had been run down anyway, as A.J. Stannah became more interested in property development. Brian Stannah could recall being taken by his grandfather to a block of flats in south London, which he owned.

Brian's other memories of A.J. include his home at 42 Ashburton Avenue, near Croydon:

A large garden at the rear contained greenhouses, the smell of tomato plants in a humid atmosphere will always remain with me. Post-war Grandpa, the entrepreneur still at 80, built three garages to provide rental income and I can still see him now, sitting on an upturned bucket laying bricks one by one, aided by a schoolboy who mixed the mortar and fetched and carried. He had a lean-to workshop beside the house with Myford lathe, pedestal drill and a brass bound case of toolmaker's tools and he prepared for my future with the monthly gift of a copy of 'Popular Mechanics' mailed from the USA which stimulated an interest in things mechanical. He did not own a car then, but Pop would speak of Grandpa's love of Renault cars, of which he had several, in the Edwardian era.

With his factory premises a ruined bombsite, little remained of the company that Joseph Stannah had created. Albert Joseph was, by now, aged 77, so we might expect the business to have been run down as he approached retirement during the 1930s.

This might have brought an end to our story, but Leslie Stannah had other ideas and, on leaving the Navy, he set about rebuilding the business.

2.37 Leslie Stannah served throughout the war and eventually attained the rank of Lieutenant Commander and Divisional Commanding Officer of HMS Duke, *the shore-based training establishment in Malvern, Worcestershire. (This photograph was taken when he was still a Lieutenant.)*

It might be more correct to say that he recreated the business from scratch. The records of the J. Stannah company during the inter-war years are very sketchy, and are non-existent after 1928. By 1945 there was very little left of the thriving enterprise that Joseph had created. What Leslie – ably supported by Jean – then achieved, through his hard work and determination to succeed, created the foundations of all that was to follow and was a key source of inspiration to their sons, Brian and Alan. The importance of this cannot be overstated. Without Leslie's will and determination, the story that will unfold over the following chapters would have been still-born in the ruins of what was by then a London bombsite.

CHAPTER THREE

1946–1960

New Foundations

'He re-created a viable business'
Alan's recollections of home life in the 1940s and 1950s
Everyone remembers the Nissen hut
We must be self-sufficient
Early post-war memories
Accident book
Preparing for the future

'HE RE-CREATED A VIABLE BUSINESS'

When Leslie Stannah was demobilised from the Navy in 1945 (or 'demobbed' as it was popularly known), he and his wife Jean returned to their pre-war home in West Wickham, Kent, with their two sons, Brian and Alan, to restart their lives together. With London in ruins and rationing even more severe than during the war, Leslie took the courageous decision to rebuild the family business from the wreckage of the old. The challenge that he faced is described in graphic detail by Brian Stannah's account of this post-war revival. This is what Brian wrote in *Elevation* magazine in 1990:

> Father … left the Service in 1945 with the rewards given by a grateful nation – a strangely shaped civvy suit, an even stranger felt hat and a small gratuity of, I believe, £300 [about £15,000 in today's money]. With these assets, the support of his wife and the handicap of, or at least the responsibility for, two young children, he set out to re-start Stannah Lifts Limited. He was 44 at the time.

Writing this now, I find it hard to describe the enormity of the task. He had no factory, no plant, no designs, no source of ready-made components, no staff. He did have a motor car which had stood on bricks for six years. He sold that, probably for less than £100, to swell his working capital and he set out to find a factory by sharing someone else's and the use of their machine tools.

He sat at the drawing board and produced designs, not just for lifts but for parts – locks, brakes, gears, pulley wheels. He then went out and knocked on doors looking for orders – and they were hard to come by. But somehow, in those years of austerity, post-war shortages and controls, he re-created a viable business.

These few words cannot begin to describe the scale of that achievement. The syllabus of a Naval Officer did not include business skills, but, after those six years, this man had quickly to adapt to being design draughtsman, factory foreman, erection supervisor, estimator, typist, salesman, wages clerk and a few others.

Although, as we have seen, by the end of the 1939–45 war little remained of the business of J. Stannah, there remained one key family asset – the freehold property at 49–51 Tiverton Street, London, SE1. This was now both a bombsite representing the ruins of the past and a potential building site supporting Leslie's hopes for the future.

3.1 Many parts of London had been razed to the ground, including A.J. Stannah's premises.

With a bulldog determination that was typical of the man, Leslie set to and started the business again. He initially set up a wire cage in the corner of a factory owned by Vaughan Lifts in Featherstone Street, London EC1. Alan Stannah said that his first memory of the lift company was a visit to Pop in this small workshop, a little area enclosed by wire mesh. Leslie then rebuilt the family business factory at Tiverton Street, near the Elephant and Castle, on the site of his father's ruined factory. The finance came from the War Damage Commission. Apparently the original building had been three storeys high, but Leslie had to make do with two. Behind 49–51 Tiverton Street was another empty site where cottages had been before they were bombed. In the 1950s Pop was able to buy this land for a nominal sum, and he laid down a concrete slab and put on it an ex-War Department Nissen hut. It was, in many ways, a very tough time to start a business. The war may have ended but the world was in a terrible state.

The freehold at that time was still owned by Pop's father, A.J. Stannah, and was encumbered by debts of about £1,800. There is evidence of a fairly tense family negotiation, resulting in an agreement between Pop and his father in a letter from Pop dated 4 July 1947. In this, he agreed to take over all liabilities, including some outstanding payments of £130 per month to A.J.'s sister, Pop's aunt Louise.

3.2 When Leslie Stannah started the company again, a War Department Nissen hut was purchased. The Nissen hut, invented and developed by a Norwegian, Peter Nissen, and his father, was a prefabricated steel structure made from a half-cylindrical skin of corrugated steel. It was relatively cheap to make and was widely used during both world wars.

The original agreement provided for A.J. to contribute to some of the legal and other outstanding costs, but whether initially agreed or not, this liability was rescinded in an amendment dated 7 March 1950 in a handwritten note in the margin of the letter. A.J.'s handwriting was still firm and clear, showing a strong family resemblance to Leslie Stannah's.

Conditions in the early post-war years were summed up by Walter Laqueur in his book, *Europe Since Hitler: The Rebirth of Europe*:

3.3 *A.J. and Edith at 42 Ashburton Avenue in the early post-war years.*

There were parades, laughter and dancing in the streets all over Europe on Victory Day, but on the morning after, Europeans began to take stock of the consequences of the war. It was a horrifying balance, enough to fill with despair even the staunchest hearts. Not since the seventeenth century had a war in Europe been fought so ferociously and caused so much destruction. Peace had now returned, but many felt, like the poet at the end of the Thirty Years War, that it was the peace of a churchyard. It had come too late. Not a few feared that Europe would never again rise from the ashes. Europe had never fully recovered from the terrible bloodbath of the first world war and its ravages; but now, in retrospect, that war seemed almost insignificant. There had been eight million victims in 1914–18; now there were four times as many. France with 620,000 victims and Britain with 260,000, had suffered less in the second world war, but the loss of life in central and eastern Europe was enormous. Poland had lost more than 20 per cent of its population (including the millions of Jews murdered), and Yugoslavia 10 per cent. Soviet losses were estimated between 12 and 20 million, German (again including civilian losses) at more than five million. Even a small country like Greece had suffered grievously.

Roy Porter in his *London, A Social History* also gives us the atmosphere in the London in which Leslie Stannah set up his business.

3.4 Demobbed soldiers being measured for their civvy suits provided free by a grateful government. After the doodle-bugs (flying bombs) the desire was for back to business as usual. Demobbed majors dusted down their brollies, and wives left munitions work and went back to the kitchen sink.

Postwar London presents an enigma. After the doodle-bugs the sigh was for 'business as usual', for peace and quiet and cosy, familiar routines, and Londoners resumed their old lifestyles as if the clock could be turned back. Demobbed majors dusted down their brollies; wives left munitions work and went back to the kitchen sink; cricket enjoyed the golden age of the Comptons and Bedsers; the Olympic Games came to London in 1948. The late 1940s and early 1950s were old London's Indian summer, when the docks still thrived and the trams sailed majestically through pea-soupers; East Enders had their knees-up at the pub and went hop-picking in August; contented commuters in Chessington tended their herbaceous borders; before variety was finally killed by television, it enjoyed its swansong at the Hackney and Deptford Empires, or Collins' at Islington.

The postwar years proved difficult, of course, with their fuel shortages, power cuts and ubiquitous queuing. Rebuilding proceeded slowly. With money short and a certain LCC puritanism in the air, reconstruction was cautious and vision rationed. If the post-1666 rebuilding was a chance missed, that judgement applies all the more to the post-1945 era. London's fabric was patched up, but no fresh start was made with respect to street plans, transport or the siting of employment. And there was no Wren.

3.5 The post-war years were very difficult. Rationing continued, in the case of meat – apart from horse-flesh! – for a full nine years, and in 1947 even bread was rationed, something not deemed necessary during the war. No wonder Winston Churchill and the Conservatives were re-elected in 1951 with their promise of a 'bonfire of controls'.

ALAN'S RECOLLECTIONS OF HOME LIFE IN THE 1940s AND 1950s

When we returned home to 116 The Grove, West Wickham, Kent, after the war my first recollection is of the local builders and decorators, Mr Aitcheson and his son, known locally as 'old and young Aitchy', pulling down our ceilings and re-plastering them after the damage caused by the flying bomb. The car in the garage was sold to provide finance for Pop's fledgling business and this was not to be replaced until the early 1950s.

Monday was washing day at the kitchen sink, with a ribbed scrubbing board with drying on an airer hoist to the kitchen ceiling over the black coke solid fuel boiler. The washing machine, when it came, was a great advance and it was many years before an electric fridge arrived.

Pop had a mile to walk to the station to catch the train to London Bridge, which was a short bus ride or walk to 'the works' at 49–51 Tiverton Street, in an area known as The Elephant and Castle.

At this time, in about 1947, I progressed to my second school to which I travelled by bus costing a tuppenny half, Brian travelling further to Whitgift School at Hayling Park, South Croydon, for a further penny – a total equivalent of about 1p in current decimal coinage. Later I joined Brian at Whitgift and we both cycled to school, a journey of about five miles, braving the Croydon tramlines that were always a hazard to cyclists and the roadworks caused by the searches for buried, unexploded German bombs.

Christmas was a great family event, shared over three days between our house and Mother's brother Billy and her two maiden sisters, our Aunts Clara and Elizabeth, who made a great effort to provide entertainment for Brian and me and our cousin David (Billy and Winnie's son). On each of these three days we had a turkey Christmas dinner, followed by opening presents on Christmas Day, tea, games and then

3.6 Alan and Brian Stannah, aged seven and eleven, in 1946 when they were living in West Wickham, Kent.

supper – and all as Brian has described without a drop of alcohol in sight.

Pop worked hard at developing the business, frequently sitting in the evening working on an estimate for a lift contract with little time for relaxation.

House decorating was definitely DIY and we all tried our hands at painting and wall papering, which was not too difficult if one persevered. One Spring a late snowfall slid off the roof which proved too much for the garage and Brian and Pop re-built this together. Brian was good with his hands and re-tiled the fireplaces fitting modern (for then) slow burning fires which, with luck, stayed in all night. This was appreciated in winter, as there was no central heating or insulation. Winters were colder then and we enjoyed sledging and later in our teens using our old cars to tow each other on skis around the local roads, which provoked mixed reactions from our neighbours.

Brian and I both owned pre-war cars and these were frequently in pieces, including in the kitchen. Mother was very supportive to us, as she believed this interest in things mechanical might eventually be of benefit to the business and we are grateful to her for her patience at such goings on.

Most people aspired to earn £5 a week [£150 a week in today's money]. We made everything ourselves and it was a pretty basic factory. For example we had to wash our hands in a bucket of hot water, the water being heated on a gas ring.

On Anderson's employment agreement of 20 April 1949 it said that during his first year he would be paid not less than 8.37d per hour (3.5p or about £1 in today's money). He would then receive 9.9d in his second year, 13.69d in the third, 15.98d in the fourth and 19.01d in the fifth, so that even by that time, his pay in today's money would be £2.40 an hour – or £115 for a 48-hour week, or £5,760 a year. Mind you, on the side of the agreement was typed:

> A merit rate bringing these rates to 10.5d, one shilling, 1s 3d and 1s 5d respectively will be paid at the employer's discretion.

Different ways, different world. In 1949 the *maximum*, not minimum, wage of a professional footballer (Stanley Matthews included) was £10 a week. In that year, Wolverhampton Wanderers beat Blackburn Rovers in the FA Cup final. The Blackburn player, Dave Whelan, broke his leg, never played football again, started his own business and is now a multi-millionaire. It's an ill wind!

John Whittlesey, another employee of the early 1950s, remembered:

> For me, life at Stannah's started on the 3rd February 1953.
>
> The first lift was 'The Tile' at the Borough High Street. It was a 6 passenger, wooden car, top drive. This was where we used a Scout barrow to carry the materials. All the lift parts were manufactured at Tiverton Street, except for the foundry mouldings. The mode of transport for carrying most parts was a dust cart that the old man hired.
>
> I'm sending you a couple of snaps of the old man's equipment which I must say in my opinion were the best in the game.
>
> Stannah's renovated seven lifts in Guy's Hospital and installed three new installations, between 1954–1970. An amusing incident this may make you laugh – we had to put a fire-proof lift in the motor works at Oxford. Well, the old man had a great big black Sunbeam and we loaded all our tools in the boot. These weighed about 2 cwt. Then Roy Lewis, myself and J. Jenkins climbed in the car. Well, the old man took off like a jet fighter. Half-way up the A4 we stopped at a Café. We had 3 teas and a coffee for me. We had only just sat down and the old man yelled let's go, so we called him 'Tin Gullet'. Well, we arrived at the main gate of the Motor Works where the old man watched us unload the car. Then him and Jenkins turned around and left us with a two mile trip dragging all that equipment up hill on a trolley. Believe me, we added a few more words to 'Tin Gullet'.
>
> The old memory starts to fade over 50 odd years. I can still remember the funny bits, but they have too many swear words to repeat. Oh yes! Just recalled one thing. I had just finished a 6 person lift at Springals in Saffron Hill. The old man turned up

with wagon. He said 'Strip the lift out, that so and so Architect won't pay'. Well, I told the Governor how long it had taken to fill that conduit with 3/029 (this was the wire size, the copper wire being coated with rubber and a type of cloth covering) and just as I was cooling down I heard the old man say 'It's all right John, leave it – he's waving a cheque.'

Yet another apprentice from the 1950s, Dave Evans, also has memories of those days:

In the early days at Tiverton Street, I recall a Stannah door operator and retiring ramp used as a test rig for the Stannah lock. The operator would close a small door panel, the retiring ramp would then operate, the prelock on the lock made and operated a bell to show the lock was functioning correctly. The lock was tested for a number of operations to ensure all was well.

In the early days we used the services of Hawkins Transport to deliver lifts to site. However I do remember the day to day method of getting equipment to site was by London Transport. 12'00" lengths of conduit were cut in two, as we were not allowed to take any item longer than 6'00" onto a London bus or tube train. Gallon cans of oil were put into bags to disguise them due to the fact oil was prohibited. I believe a door operator was returned to Tiverton Street also by London Underground.

I can remember the teamwork. One example was at Portsoken House in the Minories, where the generator had to be removed for rewind. The only problem was it was extremely large and was housed underneath an access platform under the control panel. Access was limited which meant the person working on the generator was only able to work comfortably for a very short space of time. Alan Mitchell was the fitter and Pete Lockton and myself were the apprentices. Due to the urgent timescale you came to site, donned your overalls and took your turn to dismantle the generator. I can also remember Pop dropping components at my mother's house on more than one occasion as they were needed urgently on site the next day.

Progress. When we see the Microprocessors of today, I remember the Duplex control panels of the sixties and seventies. City of London College, Kingston car park etc. But the largest of all was the duplex control panel installed at the Methodist Missionary Society, Marylebone Road. It was larger than a double wardrobe.

It was necessary to work a number of late nights (on occasions until 11.30pm). Pop would leave his office at the end of the day, drive home and then drive all the way to West Hampstead with sandwiches and flasks of tea and coffee for the fitters and apprentices working on the site. Needless to say Mrs Stannah prepared the food and drinks.

ACCIDENT BOOK

Under the Workmen's Compensation Act of 1925, employers were obliged to keep an accident book.

Full Name, Address and Occupation of Injured Workman. (1)	Signature of Injured Workman or other person making this Entry. (If the entry is made by some person acting on behalf of the Workman, the address and occupation of such person must also be given). (2)	Date when Entry made. (3)	Date of Accident. (4)	Room or Place in which Accident happened. (5)	Cause and Nature of Injury. (6)
S. Benson (Chargehand)	S. Benson (M.O.)	16-9-66	16-9-66	Workshop	Handwheel fell from chuck on right hand. Bruising.
P. Sansbury	S. Benson (M.O.)	3-10-66	3-10-66	— " —	Cut left hand (palm) whilst working radial drill (Hospital)
A. Scott - 9H1	Ascott	16/1/67	16/1/67		Hit knee on pumbine whilst moving Rolly drum
Errol Danvers	R Howard (CHd)	11/4/67	6/4/67	Royal storage, Bayswater, Nottinghill Gate	Slipped left hand in between serving lift.
	in workshop	"	"	Nottinghill Gate	or serving hatch.
B. Lawrence	S. Benson (M.O.)	6-7-67	6-7-67	Workshop	Dropped Guide Shoe Housing cut finger (sent to hospital) Crushed small finger LH. Badly gashed. 8.45. (Sent to hospital)
P. Sansbury	S. Benson (M.O.)	7-7-67	7-7-67	Workshop	Sheave fell onto lathe onto left wrist
N. Anderson	Nicholson	1-8-67	1-8-67	Workshop	Panel ran through out of right eye sent to hospital
E. DANVERS.	S. Benson (M.O.)	21-8-67	21-8-67	Workshop	Index finger R.H. caught in spindle of milling machine. Sent to hospital
O. RICHARDS	S. Benson (M.O.),	20-2-68	20-2-68	Workshop	Badly cut finger L.H. whilst working mill. 4.40. (Sent to hospital)
R. HOWARD	S. Benson (M.O.),	25-9-68	25-9-68	Workshop	Fell off step ladder. Complained of injury to back. 13.30 p.m.
Peter Whitehead	S. Benson (M.O)	21-11-68	21-11-68	Workshop.	Drill pierced between 1st & 2nd finger R.H. Sent to hospital 11·00 am
Alan LeConte	S Benson (M.O.)	5-12-68	5-12-68	Workshop	Cast Iron block fell on Left foot. (3·55 pm)
O. Richards	S. Benson (M.O.)	5-12-68	5-12-68	Workshop	Cut middle finger L.H whilst working cropper machine (2-56 pm)
R. Pritchard	S Benson (M.O)	31-1-69	31-1-69	Workshop	Crushed thumb L.H. whilst using ½ cap. drill (3·50 pm)
J. Yarwood	S Benson (M.O,)	4-3-69	4-3-69	Workshop.	Droped face plate on foot. (Left)

3.10 The Accident Book which, under the Workmen's Compensation Act of 1925, all manufacturing employers were obliged to keep.

Stannah Lifts Limited kept one initially at 47–51 Featherstone Street, London EC1, and the first entry is 22 July 1948 when Stanley Wiggett cut the second finger on his right hand. A David Banister cut his thumb on 23 August 1948. Stanley Wiggett cut his finger again on 22 September and his thumb on 9 November.

Of the people who stayed a long time with Stannah and from whom we have received reminiscences, Alan Mitchell suffered a serious injury on 19 April 1956, when it was recorded: 'Crushed Right Hand while assisting Yarwood. Moving Gate stacked in Office Entrance.' John Yarwood was one of the two skilled machinists, the other being Bob Howard who retired in March 1993 after 41 years' service. Sadly, John Yarwood suffered a heart attack while at work and, in spite of Bob Howard nobly rendering mouth-to-mouth resuscitation, died on the shopfloor.

Mitchell was back at work by November but his hand was continuing to give trouble, as illustrated by this entry on 5 November 1956: 'Right hand swelled up while using small Driller.'

George Sabourin was born in 1937 in Bermondsey, joined the British Army in 1955 and served for three years training as a motor mechanic. Returning to 'Civvy Street', he did not enjoy the pressures of the motor trade and discovered Stannah through the Soldiers, Sailors, Airmen and Families Association (SSAFA).

He also has fond memories of Pop Stannah:

One of the outstanding things that I remember about Mr Stannah Snr is the day that I came for an interview with him. I had been recommended to him from the SSAFA, a charity for ex service people which Mr Stannah Snr supported. After he had interviewed me he asked me which part of the army I had served in.

I told him that I had served in the REME and he asked me the name of my commanding officer. I told him his name was Major Fletcher and Mr Stannah Snr told me that he knew him! All the time that I knew Mr Stannah Snr I was amazed by the people that he knew.

Some of the other things I can recall are working in the iron shed [the Nissen hut] out back at Tiverton Street and running lift parts up to Guy's Hospital on a builder's hand cart. The central heating at Tiverton Street consisted of pipes off a coke boiler which had to be lit by hand each morning.

I can also remember Christmases at Tiverton Street. We all got a turkey. Mind you, Pop expected you to work pretty well to the last minute on Christmas Eve. I remember one year, John Whittlesey and I knocked off the site we were on at lunchtime on Christmas Eve and went to the local pub. Lo and behold suddenly there was the famous brolly handle round John's neck and the familiar voice, 'What are you doing here, Whittlesey?'

Sabourin confirms Pop's concern for his men:

He would turn up on site and say 'Let's go to the café.' He would then march to the front of the queue in the café and say, 'Tea and sticky buns for my men!'

Of Pop, Brian writes:

We saw little of Pop during the War although, as already said, we lived in Sussex, and near Malvern, to be near to him. I can recall one period of leave when he took us to his sailing club at Emsworth, having been a member since pre-war. Sailing followed the motor cycling and gave him much pleasure.

Post-war he had little spare time working seven days a week with drawing board and papers covering the dining table except at mealtimes. His only relaxation was walking the dog for 20 minutes or so in the evening.

We only really got together on holiday, usually spent in a rented cottage on Chichester Harbour with day sails in a 16ft Emsworth One Design, a Gunter rigged clinker built three quarter decked centreboard dinghy. Emsworth Sailing Club (to which he belonged) had a fleet of about 10 for members' use. Being the same design, but with individual quirks, they made for interesting and fun racing.

Mistral was an old wooden six metre class keelboat about 20ft on the waterline which Pop managed to buy in around 1950 – for a 'song' I would guess – which he kept at Itchenor. I don't remember the actual sailing, only filling the seams and painting whilst the hull was supported on legs on the Itchenor hard, only possible at half-tide or less, so a fairly inefficient process. Itchenor was reached by Southern Railway from East Croydon Station, bus from Chichester and a final walk of a mile or so carrying paint, materials and weekend clothes.

In his retirement, Pop bought another old wooden boat, *Tess of Teign* (believed designed by Maurice Griffiths) from somewhere in the West Country. He actually had virtually no coastal or offshore experience, which was limited to Chichester Harbour. However, he prevailed on the father of one of my friends to accompany him as crew on the trip up from the West Country to Chichester Harbour. We never knew exactly what transpired in the course of that trip, but the crew (Bert Cheswick) was white faced on arrival and I believe they didn't speak again.

Post-war in 1946, one of Pop's first acts was to de-mothball the Wolseley Hornet and convert it into working capital to help fund the regenerating business. He remained car-less until 1953, when he was able to buy a Sunbeam Talbot, a fairly roomy saloon similar in all but name to the Humber Super Snipe, large of body but woefully lacking in power from its three litre side valve engine, manufactured in about 1938.

He taught me to drive in it and then amazingly allowed me to use it largely for the benefit of the West Wickham Young Conservatives, the members of which paid scant attention to matters politic which would have distracted from more pressing social engagements, dances and pub crawls featuring more than somewhat.

Now these activities created a certain difficulty at home. After six years in the Royal Navy, Pop was known to enjoy the occasional tincture from Plymouth. His wife, Jean, who we will now call Mother had very different views on anything alcoholic. Brought up by strict Presbyterian parents in Scotland, as a child she would cross the road rather than walk past the open doors of a public house and was a teetotaller throughout her life. This abstinence was imposed on the rest of the family, so home coming from evenings out had to be deferred until the parental bedroom light was off. One feels sorry for Pop having to toe the line. Maybe a closer bond with Alan and I could have been formed had a glass of wine been shared over dinner. Wine eventually put in a guarded appearance at Christmas-time and after Alan and I had each got married. Mother affected not to notice.

Back to *Mistral* and the Autumn of 1954 or 1955. *Mistral* was to be laid up at Mill Rythe creek on Hayling Island, with Pop and I sailing her from her mooring (she had no engine). We ran her aground on a falling tide before reaching her berth, the tides having been miscalculated. The result was that the journey had to be completed under oars in the tender, a small pram dinghy about 8ft long. That too ran aground and thereafter I had to wade through the mud and tow the dinghy with Pop sitting in the stern. Chichester Harbour mud must be experienced to fully comprehend just how memorable it can be. For a start, it's deep – usually knee deep. Then when disturbed it is reminiscent of a well used pig sty on a warm day. Finally, like a wetsuit, once on it's hell to get off again. Most of the passengers on the bus changed their seats when we eventually returned to where the Sunbeam had been left earlier.

The drive home took some two hours and it was only thereafter in the course of a hot bath that I finally regained the circulation in each foot. Memorable indeed!

Alan recalls that his life-long interest in sailing arose from Pop's introduction to sailing the Emsworth One Design around Chichester Harbour from the late 1940s. Every year, Mother would pack up a trunk of our belongings and in those early years before we owned a car this would be sent 'luggage in advance' to what was then The Grange Guesthouse, which has now become the smart Millstream Hotel in Old Bosham. The EODs were Club boats which could be borrowed by Club members and we spent Pop's short holidays and the occasional weekend making our way under sail down the winding channels of Chichester Harbour to our childhood paradise of the grass covered sand dunes of East Head at the entrance of Chichester Harbour. Pop was never happier than when he was at the helm of a boat and these days gave us many happy memories of our holidays as a family together.

PREPARING FOR THE FUTURE

Brian and Alan Stannah were both prepared for their future careers with training by competitors. In those days, competition was less cut-throat, and amicable relationships existed between those at the top; and it was quite natural for sons to be trained in other companies. Brian had been apprenticed at a rival lift manufacturer, J. & E. Hall Ltd of Dartford, Kent. This is how he wrote about it in the 1999 edition of *Elevation*:

We are delighted that our apprenticeship programme in Stannah is so active. There is no substitute for the hands-on experience that such training can give. Our apprentices join us with ambitions for their future, and later in their careers their practical knowledge will be invaluable.

I recall with gratitude my own days as a not very studious 'student apprentice' in the 1950s. In those days 'competition' was a dirty word and the tempo of life was so much slower than today's. Each morning Pop and his nearest competitor, a director of J. & E. Hall Limited, met for coffee. Those were the days. Sons (and maybe daughters) were welcomed by rival firms as trainees, and Halls were a much respected firm: number three in the lift industry, and market leader in marine refrigeration equipment.

J. & E. Hall, in Dartford, Kent, were a true engineering company. They took in raw material and, though their skills, converted it into lifts and marine freezers.

Their student apprentices were able to experience the full spectrum of making things. First was the iron foundry. Totally gripping for a novice. Extremes of temperature (no heating in winter but molten iron daily). Grown-ups playing sand castles whilst moulding on the foundry floor.

I well remember the flames, smoke, smells and humour, and next day iron shapes were put out to 'weather'.

3.11 Brian Stannah, who began life in the lift world with an apprenticeship at one of his father's friendly competitors, J. & E. Hall Ltd of Dartford, Kent.

Iron castings take time to relax and discard the risk of distortion due to the extremes of heat. So they weathered, in the open, just like fresh-sawn oak logs.

However, we apprentices moved on in that hothouse of learning. Machine shops, fitting shop, coppersmiths, boiler makers, electrical controls, wood-workers and pattern makers. New abilities and aptitudes were gained from friendly craftsmen keen to pass on their skills and knowledge. Then – clean fingers and 'the drawing office'. Not an easy transition being tied to a drawing board (no CAD back then) after the relative freedom of the workshops. However, there were new disciplines and other skills to learn.

Blue overalls once more on installation, and the challenge of each new site. The first Paternoster – an endless belt of ever moving walk-in, walk-out cabins suited to multi-level offices – to be installed since the War. Paternosters were soon to be abandoned on safety grounds.

3.12 Brian Stannah would drive the fifteen miles from West Wickham to J. & E. Hall in this Austin 7. Its main tools were a hammer and nails, as the wooden parts tended to come apart in the rain.

Four happy years passed, during which the engineering skills I learnt were applied, in turn, to a BSA Bantam and a Triumph 250 motorbike, then an Austin 7 followed by an Austin 7 'Special' with hardboard panelled body which swelled in the rain, necessitating hammer and nails as extras in the toolkit.

In 1958 Alan Stannah left school to start his period of apprenticeship training. While at school, Alan recalls:

My earliest ambitions were to command a Destroyer in the Royal Navy and later to fly with the Royal Air Force. However, perhaps due to an upbringing of taking bicycles and cars to pieces and the day-to-day influence of our family engineering background, I was happy to plan my future in our family business.

I could not help but grow up with an interest in engineering. The bureau in the living room was full of blueprints of lift components, winding gears, V-sheaves, brakes etc., although at that time I would not have known the names of the individual components, just that they were complicated looking engineering drawings and always in the characteristic blue of the blueprint. Other influences were books

3.13 Alan Stannah in a Tiger Moth. As he said later: 'My earliest ambitions were to command a Destroyer in the Royal Navy and later to fly with the Royal Air Force.'

that I was given by Grandpa Stannah. 'The Young Electrician' sparked my interest in things electrical and *Odhams Motor Manual* gave me an early insight into the workings of motor cars. He also subscribed to 'Popular Mechanics' for Brian, an American magazine that we both read avidly.

Motorbikes and old cars were part of our lives around this time. Brian started with a string of motorbikes, which I was not allowed so my first vehicle was a V-twin JAP-engined Morgan three wheeler – just as dangerous as any motorbike. Both Brian and I owned Austin Sevens and Riley Nines. I remember working with Brian late one night reassembling the engine on a Wolseley Hornet Eustace Watkins Special. I started to build a 750 Formula racing car based on Austin Seven components, but this came to a fiery end after a late night cigarette end was thrown out of Brian's window and landed on the car below, causing a flaming conflagration in the small hours of the morning. This probably saved my life, as it was likely to have been a most dangerous contraption. I was secretly relieved, although I don't recall telling Brian this at the time.

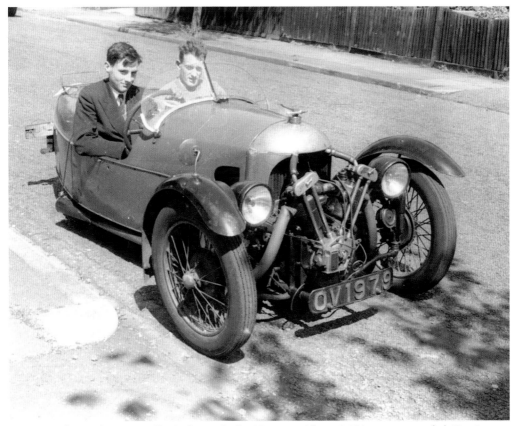

3.14 Alan and Brian in Alan's three-wheeler Morgan with an 1,100cc, water-cooled, V-twin, JAP engine – 'as dangerous as any motorbike'!

Perhaps the most enjoyable part of my schooldays arose from my involvement with the combined Cadet force in which every Tuesday we dressed up in military uniforms and on Tuesday afternoons followed a range of activities associated with one of the Services. After a compulsory first year in the Army section which was enlivened by firing blank cartridges and throwing thunder flashes, I opted to transfer to the Royal Air Force section which included learning the principles of flight and the occasional practice of this in the school glider, which was launched by a huge elastic band across the school playing fields. I managed a short hop in this up to a height of about six feet, although another pupil managed to achieve nearer 20 feet thereafter descending rapidly tail first before emerging from a pile of splintered wreckage. Croydon Airport was not far from the school and it was there that I learnt to fly a Tiger Moth, having gained a flying scholarship through the CCF from a generous Royal Air Force. My account of one of my days during this period of flying training later appeared in *Elevation* magazine in 1995. An extract from this is given below:

I recall a fine summer's day, which I see from my log book was 18th April 1958 when as a Cadet in the CCF I arrived at the Surrey Flying Club at Croydon Airport for my triangular cross-country flight. I was later than I had intended, as my old V twin JAP-engined Morgan had been more reluctant to start than usual. I leapt out, taking care to miss the hot exhaust pipe which ran down the side of the Morgan's cockpit, grabbed my bag containing my air cadet's uniform and legged it for the Flying Club office. I didn't make it without being spotted. 'Stannah' bawled the CFI, 'you're late!' 'Cadets Bell and Praeskl have gone already and your 'plane, Yankee November, is u/s, so you'll have to wait.'

It was the day scheduled for our triangular cross-country flight from Croydon to Lymne and Shoreham, returning to Croydon, part of our training programme for our pilot's licence on which we were lucky enough to be enrolled.

I resigned myself to a long wait, as I lay and dozed on the grass outside the flight office. Time passed and I was awoken by the sound of the telephone. Through the open window I heard snippets of conversation. It was Cadet Bell at Lymne with a broken propeller. Taxi-ing to refuel he had hit the petrol pump. Oh dear!

The CFI vented his wrath on poor Bell, who would have to await a new propeller which would be sent by road. The sun shone and I dozed again.

Again the telephone rang. This time it was Praeskl, who was under a cloud already having been reported recently by a BEA Captain for flying inverted in an airway, making his offence worse by waving as he passed. He had also lost his way and flown low over an abandoned railway station in an endeavour to read the name. It was now a poultry farm and the infuriated owner had complained at the resulting one thousand broody hens that had gone off laying because of his low flying antics.

Praeskl was now at Shoreham and likely to stay there. He had stalled in from 20 feet and now his undercarriage was no longer as designed. More wrath from the CFI.

My turn came at last, my trip marked only by the sad sight of Tiger Moth relics along the way. On my return to Croydon, I bid farewell to a strangely pleasant CFI and sat in the Morgan in the evening sunshine to reflect on an eventful day.

At school I studied the science subjects and also metalwork, which took precedence over French (which, owing to somewhat moderate 'A' Level results, closed the doors to University). This was no bad thing as through his contacts at The National Association of Lift Makers, Pop arranged for me to undertake a four year period of industrial training with Hammond and Champness Limited, at that time a major lift manufacturing company.

This was quite a change from lazy days at public school. I had to present myself at their factory in Walthamstow, North London, before 7.30 a.m. each Monday morning – which meant a very early start from our home in West Wickham. With my new suit of overalls, I was given a job in the control panel test shop where I became a member of the small team testing the lift control panels before these were despatched to site. This was a wonderful opportunity and gave me an early insight into the workings of lift controls from the simplest goods lifts up to control systems for banks of three or four interconnected high-speed passenger lifts.

Nobby Clark and Ernie Harrison were the control panel testers and I remember their patience in teaching a rather precocious youngster the ropes.

After six months I transferred to work as a Tester's Mate with one of the senior Lift Testers, Frank Hollingsworth. Frank's jobs were all around London. Frank knew the whereabouts of all the tea shops and we used to meet for a cup of tea first before starting work on-site. I worked with Frank for 18 months, including the final tests on Hammonds' first quadruplex bank of four lifts, three of them with gearless winding machines. When the Tester was on holiday, I was given the job of wiring up Ernie, a central control unit for all four lifts. With this work completed, like the Sorcerer's Apprentice, I switched them all on for the first time and soon had them answering all calls to all 18 floor levels, with the lifts flying up and down the lift-shafts – the motors roaring, doors opening and closing as never before. The Site Foreman burst into the motor room to shout at me 'The lifts have gone mad!' I decided it was time to call it a day and switched the lifts off. On the Tester's return from holiday, the company top brass solemnly assembled in recognition of this significant company milestone – the first time four lifts had been switched on together (or so they thought). I also enjoyed a spell with another tester, Joe Caulfield, testing a bank of three lifts at Halifax College, which allowed a weekend visit to Aintree for the British Grand Prix in which Stirling Moss and Tony Brooks were competing. It was all very different from the Formula One racing of today. All in all, this was wonderful experience and I had the time of my life.

These practical apprenticeships for Brian and Alan gave them firm foundations for their future careers. They were, as in the family tradition, true hands-on lift engineers. What follows shows the value to the business of the training they received during their periods of apprenticeship.

By the early 1960s the business was on a sound, if slender, footing. Post-war reconstruction in London provided opportunities for small companies to grow, but margins were slim and success by no means assured. However, in their favour was the service, repair and call-out work that provided an ongoing income stream following each new lift installation, which was to prove to be their salvation and in following years a springboard to later success.

The design work involved in creating a range of specialist lift components was substantial and gave the company its identity as a true lift-maker and manufacturer, fully justifying the company's membership of NALM, the National Association of Lift Makers. Pop was contemptuous of anything less. He used to say that there were lift manufacturers, lift suppliers and lift mongers – and was proud to have established his company on a firm manufacturing footing.

Stannah's technical strengths at that time lay in the range of winding gears, brakes and door locks they developed; one might say they were the best in the industry but with a cost to match. This equipment successfully recreated and improved on the designs and equipment of Joseph Stannah and was based on sound engineering principles. An example of this was Pop's insistence that his winding gears should have only two main bearings, to ensure correct main shaft bearing alignment without the risk of main shaft breakage that can arise from the misalignment that is possible with three-bearing designs. In this, Pop followed the lead set by Joseph Stannah, who it will be remembered was earlier described as 'an extremely able and inventive engineer'.

By this time the requirements of the market for new lifts were changing, with a greater emphasis on passenger lifts with power-operated doors with new and challenging technical complexities. As the company entered the new decade there were the first signs of troubled times ahead, as the company's slender technical and financial resources were stretched to the limit and eventually to breaking point.

CHAPTER FOUR

1961–1973

CRISIS AND RECOVERY

COSTS SPIRALLING

We have already seen that Leslie 'Pop' Stannah could not resist going after new business wherever it was available. In 1960 this led him to accept contracts to put lifts into a series of high-rise blocks of flats being built by Birmingham City Council. This is how Brian Stannah explained the problems that ensued:

> After leaving school in 1953, I spent a year at college but was a terrible student. The only thing I learnt was how to play bridge. Then, after a four year student apprenticeship, from which I gained so much knowledge, I joined the business in 1958. Shortly after, the company hit hard times. Through employing a salesman paid partly by commission who had also, I believe, a hand in the estimating, the company had

4.1 A tower block in Birmingham being built in the 1950s. A major contract with Birmingham City Council proved to be too big and difficult for the company.

obtained contracts for a large number of lifts to be installed in high-rise blocks of flats in Birmingham and badly under-estimated costs. It also found difficulty in recruiting skilled labour and did not envisage the rough usage that the lifts would receive in service. The company ran out of money. I remember that the contractors were A.J. Bryant and Robert M. Douglas. One of the problems was that the rest of the economy was booming and this included the car factories around Birmingham, and we could not get skilled labour.

George Sabourin also remembers the council flats contract in Birmingham in 1960–61:

When Pop took me up in his car, I had nowhere to stay so he simply knocked on the doors of houses nearby until he persuaded someone to put me up for the night.

Sabourin is not a fan of modern Health and Safety.[1] He can remember when Stannah bought Southern Lifts and he, as the service engineer covering the south

---

1 We should make it clear that Stannah take Health and Safety very seriously and try to make sure that the health and safety of their employees, customers and suppliers run through everything they do. One example is that in any company meeting with a formal agenda, Health and Safety is the number one item on that agenda.

of England, was given a list of their service contracts in the south. One that he needed to visit was Tesco in Falmouth. As well as servicing the lift, the contract also covered servicing the roller shutters on the loading bay.

'Right,' he said to the shop manager, 'where's the ladder?'

'We don't have a ladder.'

Not to be outdone, Sabourin piled up some crates and put a dustbin on top and serviced the shutters.

Alan Stannah's apprenticeship at Hammond and Champness had progressed to a short period in the factory:

I remember, among other things, assembling the huge spring buffers that were fitted under the lifts to soften the impact should the lift overrun and also hand power driving units. I learnt to cut keyways in bronze bearings and gained a good introduction to the use of hand tools and general fitting work.

At that time there were signs of industrial unrest and it was thought better that I should move out of the factory, so I transferred into the mechanical drawing office. There we worked on serried ranks of drawing boards under the beady eye of our section leader, who would check our drawings for errors. I never ceased to be amazed how quickly he spotted my mistakes, although once an error slipped through and some huge multiple door frames proved incapable of assembly on-site requiring expensive modifications. I kept my head down for the next few weeks.

Stannah Lifts Limited was going through difficult times then. A major contract in Birmingham had proved a bridge too far and a sacrificial lamb was needed to placate the client.

I was released from my apprenticeship at Hammond and Champness for about a month while I worked on the lifts all around Birmingham. I was probably sent so that there was a member of the Stannah family facing the flak. Although the contract was probably beyond the management resources of the company at that time, there were two problems that caused major upsets that were quite outside our control. For some reason best known to themselves, the technical experts within Birmingham City Council had specified no-volt coils on the Ellison circuit breakers. The problem with these was that an intermittent failure or a drop in voltage of the electrical supply caused the lift to trip out, trapping users and causing massive inconvenience as the circuit breakers did not reset when the supply was reinstated – possibly seconds later.

Another problem was that the City Council specified safety edges on all landing doors, which was not a usual feature. The safety edges installed at that time were rubber extrusions and the manufacturer used lamp black as a lubricant in the extrusion process. Due to the number of landing door safety edges used in parallel, this was sufficient to allow a conducting path across the safety edges causing intermittent failures. One of my jobs was to replace these safety edges with an improved design. Both of these problems were outside our control and both caused us significant cost and delay and probably contributed substantially to the downfall of the business.

4.2 Brian's tuned-up A35 on a camping holiday with Jenny.

An amusing episode was that the transport I had been given was Brian's tuned up A35 which had huge aluminium trumpets on its twin SU carburettors, giving quite a startling performance. I had previously blown this up once already on my way to meeting Jackie (now my wife) for our first date after falling into bad ways against a very hot Mini finally knocking out the big ends on the A3 Horndean straight. Having rebuilt the engine, it was now entrusted to me again. As we arrived in Birmingham the engine started knocking horrendously. Thinking I had knocked out the big ends again, I sent for replacements and fitted them after jacking the car up and dropping the sump in a car park – alas with no improvement. I later found that the crank shaft was broken, but amazingly it still ran.

A Stannah Lifts Limited employee who worked with me in Birmingham at that time was Bobby Lee, later to be a Director of The National Association of Lift Makers (NALM), later renamed The Lift and Elevator Industry Association (LEIA). Bobby's father was the Duke of Edinburgh's personal chauffeur and bodyguard and he lived in Buckingham Palace. After a long journey home from Birmingham in thick fog with the engine knocking like a kettle drum, we arrived outside Buckingham Palace in the small hours of the morning only to find that Bobby Lee had forgotten his security pass.

It was too much trouble to explain this to the guards, so I bunked him over the wall and we never heard any more about it.

After this month away I returned to Hammond and Champness in Walthamstow where I finished my time with them working for Gerald Hammond under Les Gilbert in the electrical drawing office. Once again this was wonderful experience and gave me an insight into the design of lift control circuits, for which there seemed to be a never ending demand for endless variations including control circuits for the wide range of lift drive systems that were then common, as described in the following resume.

LIFT DRIVE SYSTEM DEVELOPMENTS

In Chapter One we described early mechanical and water hydraulic drive systems. By the time of my training at Hammond and Champness, the old water powered hydraulic lifts had largely been replaced by traction machines driven by various types of electric motors powered from the three phase electrical mains supply.

These could be single speed, squirrel cage, solid rotor designs with a fearsome jerk on starting due to the rising torque characteristic, coupled with poor floor levelling on stopping. The Bull Super Silent motor had a sophisticated solid rotor that gave maximum torque at starting and thus a smoother ride and more accurate floor levelling.

Pole changing motors, in effect two stators giving different speeds using a common solid rotor, were a common and more economical solution.

Eddy brakes were occasionally used in conjunction with tandem motors to give even more precise control of deceleration prior to stopping. These were powered by a DC supply usually derived from a mercury arc rectifier in the lift motor room. These flashed and sparked with a weird purple light, casting flickering shadows over the resistance banks and the oil dashpot controlled contactors that governed the various stages of speed control – a fascinating and magical scene.

More modern and sophisticated speed control was achieved by Ward Leonard DC control with the incoming mains supply driving motor generator (MG) sets that gave a DC output to the DC lift motors. The MG sets ran largely continuously so the supply was always available, although if the lift traffic was low they could be shut down to save electricity with the penalty of a delay while the MG set ran up to speed. On a cold Winter's day it was good to find a job in a multiple lift motor room, with perhaps four MG sets running in a steady whine – there was always somewhere to warm a cold posterior.

Traction drive was virtually universal at that time, although there were rumours of a growing trend to hydraulic drive in the USA. As is not uncommon, this trend would follow some years later in the UK.

Usually the traction Vee sheave was driven by the electric motor through a worm geared reduction drive, but a few high traffic lifts operating at around two metres per second were driven by direct gearless machines with the slow speed DC motor coupled directly to the driving sheave which was commonly U-grooved with a double wrap of the ropes around a wrap sheave to ensure adequate traction.

Forty years were to pass during which time the hydraulic lift drive blossomed and fought for precedence with the traction competition, until finally smaller gearless drives were to replace the geared traction arrangement.

This and the parallel developments as stairlift drive systems followed an equivalent evolution are described in later chapters.

This was how Malcolm Cogan remembered the difficult times of the Birmingham City Council contract:

A new salesman joined the company and sold a large contract for a lot of new lifts in Council flat tower blocks in Birmingham. This involved new designs to meet council specifications and Ken Williams who had taken over from Mr Garrett as chief draughtsman was overwhelmed. The result was a disaster with equipment not functioning to specification and installation costs spiralling out of control.

The financial situation of the Company became desperate in 1961, with most staff on Tuesday and Wednesday having to call on customers to collect overdue payments so that wages could be paid on Thursday. The strange thing is everything seemed to go back to normal on Friday and Monday.

I'm ashamed to say I was a rat who left the sinking ship. I had an interview with Otis and was asked what salary I was looking for. I promptly said I was hoping for four figures and after waiting outside was offered £1,000 p.a., £200 more than I received at Stannah.

Pete Lockton who, you will recall, had joined Stannah in 1958, also remembered the drama:

Some of the blocks of flats were eight storeys and some 16 storeys. I went up and down from London with a senior fitter but then was sent back to a contract for a lift in the West London Hospital. The problem was that, because of our financial difficulties, necessary materials were not being supplied. Then we were told that the company had collapsed. However, it immediately started again as Stannah Lifts Services and I carried on to complete the job at the hospital.

In the event the company was most fortunate that Brian Stannah had seen the collapse coming and together with their accountant, John King of Duncan King and Partners in Croydon, had suggested to Pop that they should move their lift service contracts to a new company, Stannah Lifts Services Ltd. The service contracts stimulated payments quarterly in advance and this provided the capital, albeit small, for business to get going again, based initially on maintenance and repair. Without this far-sighted thinking the company would probably not exist today. Gradually the company resumed the making of lifts. Brian particularly

CERTIFICATE OF INCORPORATION

ON CHANGE OF NAME

No. 942647

Whereas

BILTHAM LIMITED

was incorporated as a limited company under the
COMPANIES ACTS, 1948 TO 1967,

on the **19TH NOVEMBER, 1968**

And whereas by special resolution of the Company and with the approval
of the Board of Trade it has changed its name

Now therefore I hereby certify that the Company is a limited company
incorporated under the name of

STANNAH LIFTS (SOUTHERN) LIMITED

Given under my hand at London the **24TH JANUARY, 1969.**

Assistant Registrar of Companies

C.172

*4.3 The Certificate of Incorporation of Stannah Lift Services in 1969
– a seminal document in the history of the company.*

remembers previous clients the Sheineman family, who were engaged in property and the rag trade in Hackney, giving them a contract for four lifts in premises they owned in Old Street, East London. Brian Stannah said later: 'I have always believed that John Sheineman knew he was throwing us a lifeline and will always be grateful.'

Alan continues:

> Following the troubles in Birmingham, the company had gone into liquidation shortly before I joined and, with Brian's help, Pop had reformed the company on a very small basis. In those early days we really were working on a shoestring. On one occasion I asked Pop, 'Who are those men in suits in the factory?', to which he responded, 'They are the Bailiffs.' Somehow we just squeezed by. On one occasion with no money in the Bank, I spent my own savings to buy a set of ropes which allowed a contract to be completed and a cheque to be cashed. On another occasion we took a rush contract and Alan Mitchell and I worked all night to recommission a lift and receive a cheque from a grateful customer. By such methods we kept the wolf from the door.

Brian was now joined by Alan and together they gradually took over the running of the business while Pop, though he never formally retired, took more of an advisory role. For example, he remained active at the National Association of Lift Makers (NALM).

Recalling the earlier family history, there is a constant thread: the long sustaining marriages of Brian and Alan's forebears – Solomon and Elizabeth, Joseph and Elizabeth, Albert and Edith, and Leslie and Jean. Brian had married Jennifer Blackmore (whose great uncle was R.D. Blackmore, the author of *Lorna Doone*) in 1963. They first met when Jenny was fifteen and married immediately following her graduation from Reading University. Some five years later, Alan had wooed and married Jacqueline Harrison, elder daughter

4.4 On 7 August 1963, Brian Stannah married Jennifer Blackmore, whose great uncle, R.D. Blackmore, had written Lorna Doone.

4.5 On 12 October 1968, Alan Stannah married Jacqueline Harrison.
L to R: Brian Stannah, Leslie and Jean Stannah, Alan and Jacqueline Stannah, Connie Harrison,
Jacqueline's sister Gill, Tom Harrison. In front of Alan is Caroline O'Hagan.

of Tom Harrison and his wife Connie, two people of immense charm and character. During the Second World War, Harrison had been a prisoner of war in Stalag Luft III, where the famous Douglas Bader was also a prisoner before he escaped, was recaptured and sent to Colditz Castle. Paul Brickhill, the Australian author who wrote the biography of Bader, *Reach for the Sky*, and *The Great Escape*, was also a prisoner in Stalag Luft III.

These are Alan's recollections of joining Stannah Lifts Limited on completion of his period of apprenticeship:

After four very happy years, the time came for me to join Stannah Lifts Limited which I found to be in a small workshop in a backstreet of The Elephant and Castle off Newington Causeway, with a collection of machine tools downstairs and the various offices on the first floor.

The atmosphere was somewhat dusty and dirty, we couldn't afford office cleaners in those days. Brian and Pop were at opposite ends of the building arguing over who had first bite of *The Industrial Daily News* (the *Industrial News* was an information news-sheet which listed planning applications as they were made to the country's local councils. Brief details of the type of building and location were given and the information was of value to the sales departments of companies whose products were sold to the construction industry). I was put into the drawing office and told to get on with it, which must have been quite difficult for Roy Sturt and John Geldard, who suddenly had this upstart thrust into their midst.

In those days we made all sorts of lifts, depending on what enquiries came in and what the customer wanted, with no attempt at standardisation. We made goods lifts, passenger lifts, bed lifts and the occasional motor car lift. These latter were quite complicated, requiring pick-up in all four corners through an intricate arrangement of gearing. Getting this arrangement right sometimes proved too much of a challenge, on one occasion resulting in one end of the lift going up while the other went down, requiring a hasty re-design.

We made gearboxes, brakes, door locks, door operators, retiring cams, door couplers, selector machines, contactors, relays, push-buttons, indicators, car gate contacts, control panels, ultimate limits – in fact, the complete range of lift components and all in minute numbers, all achieved in our small workshop.

KINDNESS AND CONCERN

Dave Evans had joined Stannah Lifts as an apprentice lift engineer in December 1958 and, like others, remembers Pop for his bowler hat and brolly. However, he also remembers him for his kindness and concern for those who worked for him. Evans noted that it was a characteristic inherited by Pop's sons, Brian and Alan, and he experienced it when, as branch manager in the Bristol office in the 1980s, he had the misfortune to suffer from ME. Evans noted that they were both very understanding. He also noted that when either of the Stannahs visited the Bristol office they knew the name of every employee.

Evans's long service with Stannah showed the wide scope of the lifts the company installed and serviced. He could remember, from the 1960s, two lifts in the City of London College, and lifts in the homeopathic hospital in Great Ormond Street and in the anatomy department in Guy's Hospital, used for moving corpses for dissection by the students.

Most of the installations Evans worked on in the 1960s were in London, but there was one at the Jaguar car plant in Brown's Lane, Coventry, as well as one in the Triumph TR7 factory in Speke, Liverpool, one of these with a double-decker lift car design allowing two levels to be served at the same time.

Alan Stannah well recalls a big lift in Beck and Pollitzer, the exhibition stand company in West Hampstead, and the trouble caused by it.

In late 1963/4 we installed a large goods lift for Beck and Pollitzer at a site in West Hampstead. There was I recall a deadline to complete the installation, but a problem developed where the gearbox (Northern Engineering) was overheating.

4.6 Don McCulloch, a Stannah employee, with 'Pop' Stannah on a company day out in 1967.

This lift was very large for its load capacity. I believe it was intended for moving large but lightweight stage scenery. It was conventional to size the motor according to the load to be carried, but when commissioned the lift motor was drawing too high a running current. It was clearly overloaded and resulted in overheating. We had never experienced this before and lengthy investigations failed to produce a solution. In the end it became obvious that there was nothing wrong with the equipment. It was just that with the very large lift car for a given load rating, the frictional losses were far higher than usual and the problem was solved by fitting a larger driving motor.

The lift had been specified by specialist lift consultants, who did not prove to be much help in sorting out the problem. At one stage they insisted on a series of watt meter tests which were duly carried out and the readings solemnly recorded and noted and, with much sage nodding of heads, approved. Unfortunately they had omitted to take account of a scale factor of times four on the meter readings. The figures were multiplied by four and again noted and sagely approved. I wondered what sort of an error might have been necessary before the figures would have been queried. My well known reservation concerning the use of Consultants (admittedly frequently unjustified) possibly stems from this experience.

This was a time of transition from the equipment we had inherited from Pop as we took our first sometimes faltering steps towards new production methods and processes. Mistakes were an inevitable part of this. I have always believed that mistakes are permissible, provided one learns from the experience and, indeed, I learnt a great deal.

I learnt the hard way that saving a penny can frequently cost a Pound. Sometimes these Pounds were my own time spent on-site sorting out problems of my own making. One such contract, our first duplex pair of lifts with our own control panel in Kingston car park, is etched through my memory. However, I learnt from this that all problems have a logical cause and a logical solution. Also, that problems are bullies if you let them be, but are cowards that run away if faced up to and tackled head on.

I also learnt that it was false pride and following a blind alley in making and designing our own components in penny quantities when there were proprietary suppliers available to us offering first class components at competitive prices.

These were lessons I learnt the hard way that have stayed with me all my working life. These were not restricted to technical matters, as the following account will show.

OF MICE AND MEN

We are fortunate that over the early years of the development of the company we experienced few problems with labour relations, although from time to time situations did arise that required careful handling.

In practice these turned out for the best, as we learnt lessons from each occasion – in particular that the bolshy workforce that the Press loved to revel in was largely the product of poor management and, provided areas of difficulty were understood and handled carefully, we have benefitted from the interest and commitment of our personnel, which we have greatly appreciated.

One situation was presented to me by Ken Wilkinson, a maintenance fitter who took exception over a lift breakdown caused by dead mice in a lift pushbutton box. Ken was vehement – he was employed to service lifts, not deal with dead mice. They were not his mice, he wasn't going to have to clean up rotten dead mice, etc., etc., for half an hour, ending with 'and what are you going to do about it?!'.

There was probably a better and more skilled response, but I said something like I understood and sympathised with his problem and suggested that he use his good judgement, following which, Ken being the good sort he was, that was the last I heard of it.

Ken was also very keen that we employ Mates to work alongside the Fitters. This ran contrary to company practice at that time which relied on apprentices, as our conventional wisdom then was that mates would just cause trouble. Using apprentices gave us a steady stream of newly qualified Fitters, as the apprentices completed their training but, as time went by, this developed into an escalating geometric progression resulting in overstaffing.

Ken was adamant that the answer was to employ Mates, with the added advantage that they would not be off one day a week at college.

I was squeezed between these two firmly held views, but eventually with the apprentice situation getting out of hand I decided to take on a couple of Mates to keep Ken quiet and risk the consequences. They started the following Monday and I waited for trouble to ensue. As the weeks passed, all remained calm and the work got done without interruption. Mates, as it turned out, were a good thing. In fact, I should have known better as I'd worked with Mates during my site training and found them to be great lads and that many Mates progressed to Improver and eventually Fitter, with years of valuable experience behind them.

Ken Wilkinson later retired after 31 years' service with the company and I will always remember his good judgement and advice to me all those years ago.

KEEPING THE WHEELS TURNING

Alan also recalls that one of the joys of running a small business is the wide variety of tasks that have to be undertaken:

On one day repairs might be a bit slack, so we grabbed the pile of maintenance reports and turned them into quotations to our customers who before long then turned them into orders and work for our repair teams and a steady cash-flow.

Our sales team then was just Pop and Brian. Later we were joined by Len Rogers, but until then if orders were short I would take myself off to Planning Offices along the South Coast to drum up enquiries. I was a very green salesman, but every order counted and it gave me a very well rounded experience. By such means we kept the wheels of business turning.

Another lesson I learnt then was that the fastest way to lose money was failing to invoice our customers for completed work.

I put a wet towel round my head and checked the invoicing records of every small repair job over the previous two to three years and then every breakdown – and, hey presto, out popped about £3,000 – a King's ransom in those days.

We were also hands on with painting and decorating in the offices and also with building the new extension which was sometimes a precarious experience due to the rather unorthodox methods adopted by the very Irish builder named Clancy.

There is much to be said for a good grounding in running a small business where taking care of every penny can make the difference between survival and failure and, as the company grows, these lessons remain as important as ever.

Another member of our changing cast of players was Alan Godley, who started work for Stannah when they acquired the Eastbourne-based firm, Southern Lifts Ltd, in the 1960s. Here are some of his memories:

The first time I met Mr A. [as Godley always referred affectionately to Alan Stannah] – having not long joined Stannah's, I was working in Haywards Heath when an orange sports car arrived, and out jumped a sprightly young man who proceeded down the path.

113

By the side of the building where I was working there was a 3ft high fence just before a gate that led into the building. With the grace of a gymnast Mr A. put one hand on the fence and vaulted over – completely unaware that on the other side there was a drop of at least six feet.

Luckily he landed on a level path, and with great presence of mind he gave the comment: 'Marks out of Ten?'

One occasion that brings a smile to my face, and gives a perfect example of the quality of the personnel that Stannah's employed, happened when I had just been promoted to Tester.

I was getting strange readings from my hydraulic pump, so I phoned Peter Lockton for help. He immediately said that the readings were because the motor had been wired in Star instead of Delta. I told Peter not to be silly as this was an elementary mistake and I had checked that as a matter of routine. Peter calmly told me to check it again. I told him I wasn't that stupid!

Three minutes later, eating large amounts of humble pie, I had to ring Peter back and confirm that indeed he was right, the motor had been wired wrong, and that I was that stupid.

It was typical of Peter, and all the other members of the Stannah team that I worked with, that they never made me or any of my colleagues look or feel silly, when we had made an elementary or stupid mistake.

I also received my first ever SELETA [South East London Engineering Training Association] Certificate. For me, it reminds me of the moment when I realised that working for Stannah – I was thought of as a person with a name, and not just a number on a Payroll.

Another new recruit at this time was John Bovis, who joined Stannah Lift Services Ltd in 1966 as Chief Draughtsman. He had been working at Express Lifts and had also worked previously for Bennie Lifts.

Alan recalls:

The technical resources of the company at that time were very slender, especially in the Drawing Office which was staffed by keen but relatively inexperienced apprentices. I found it was necessary to work late into the evenings checking their work and eventually the pressure took a toll on my health, a warning signal that could not be ignored.

Going back to my time in the mechanical drawing office at Hammond and Champness, the draughtsman on the drawing board next

4.7 John Bovis, the company's Chief Draughtsman, worked with Alan Stannah to improve the design of the stairlifts, drawings of which Brian Stannah had brought back from the company Jan Hamer, in Holland.

to mine was John Bovis. Now things were beginning to get busy and I needed a chief draughtsman. I travelled up to Essex to see John late one evening and asked him if he would join us, which was the start of a great partnership.

John remembered that there were about twenty people working at Stannah, and that Pop was still very much in charge. He recalled: 'We would quote for any job and we made everything ourselves.'

Alan remembers:

In addition to our interest in engineering, John and I also shared a common enthusiasm for racing our sailing dinghies, John having built his own boats in which he had won two National Championships.

During the 1960s I spent most Summer weekends racing a range of dinghies, starting with a very old International 14 I shared with Brian. This was followed by an Osprey and later two 505s which gave exciting sailing with spray flying from these fast planing dinghies, frequently with Jackie hanging on the trapeze wire. Our racing was mostly in Chichester Harbour, but occasionally we towed away to venues along the south coast and sometimes as far afield as La Rochelle in France and the European Championships in Copenhagen. I discovered years later that Dan Knape of Kalea (our distributor in Sweden) also raced a 505 in these Championships.

We were not very successful, but we had a lot of fun.

Duncan LeFeuvre, apprenticed to Stannah in 1969, and who enjoyed a long and distinguished career with the company, first building up the Microlifts division and eventually being appointed Managing Director of that division and then widening his experience when also appointed Managing Director of the Lifts division, has some interesting recollections of Pop Stannah. In a letter to Brian Stannah, he wrote:

I remember with clarity meeting your father for the first time with Norman Anderson in 1969 at Parsons [part of Reyrolle Parsons, eventually part of Northern Engineering as it merged with Clarke Chapman in 1977 and finally taken over by Rolls-Royce in 1989 in Erith where I was to be plucked from over 100 apprentices to be transferred to Stannah Lifts. It was quite a transition to come from being one in some 3,000 people to one in a few dozen.

In my early days of apprenticeship ... I remember with some affection how Pop would arrive at the Elephant and Castle, after a long daily journey from Chichester, full of energy, dressed in his bowler hat and carrying an umbrella. He was always polite, happy, courteous, caring and inspirational.

I remember one event at Christmas time in 1971 which quite took me by surprise. He used the mistletoe as an excuse to kiss all the girls – I don't mean a peck on the cheek, but a full embrace with the sometimes reluctant female slightly bent over his left arm! [Wouldn't get away with that in 2017, Pop!]

ALWAYS HAD SOMETHING TO SAY

David Fazakerley, the Managing Director of LEIA until 2010 (the Lift and Escalator Industry Association, formerly the National Association of Lift Makers, NALM), could remember Leslie 'Pop' Stannah very well. Stannah Lifts Ltd joined NALM in 1951 and Pop attended his first meeting on 12 October of that year.

At the NALM Annual General Meeting on the same day, the Chairman 'extended a cordial welcome to Mr L.N. Stannah whose company, Stannah Lifts Ltd, had joined the Association'.

It is not recorded that Pop made any comment on this, but at the Council Meeting of 16 January 1952 the Advisory Committee agreed that for the London area the skilled hourly rate should be raised from 7s 8d (38.3p) to 8s 4d (41.67p) and for a mate from 6s 2d (30.83p) to 6s 10d (34.16p). In today's money we need to multiply by 25, so 30p then would be £7.50 and 40p would be £10.

Fazakerley recalled that Pop was anything but a passive member but rather someone who always had something to say. For example, at the NALM Council Meeting (Pop did not take long to be elected to serve on the Council) on 4 July 1957, he was reported as saying that he wished to draw the Council's attention to the cases where his firm had lost maintenance contracts owing to other members approaching the clients with quotations which he felt were quite uneconomic. He felt that this was a matter that did not do the industry or the Association as a whole any good, and he was grateful to the Chairman for allowing the matter to be ventilated at the Council.

Appointed to serve on the Advisory Committee, the following examples show the contribution that Pop made until his retirement from the Council in about 1973.

At the Council meeting on the 5th January 1960, Mr Stannah asked whether any action could be taken to avoid wastage in skilled labour by call-up for National Service, when there was such a critical shortage of such personnel, particularly when it was known that they were not being usefully employed by the services. Mr Stannah had pursued this matter through an MP who had expressed the view that the War Office would not countenance any release of servicemen on these grounds alone.

At the meeting on 6 October 1961:

Mr Stannah expressed regret that owing to extreme pressure of business he would be unable to stand for election to the advisory committee for the coming year and therefore to continue as vice-chairman. It was the desire of the meeting to record members' regret that Mr Stannah had been occasioned to withdraw from the elections and expressed the hope that Mr Stannah would again be able to resume his active work in the Association at a later date.

4.8 Leslie and Jean Stannah. He may have handed the business over to his two sons, but he continued to make a valuable contribution at the National Association of Lift Makers.

This he clearly did, as, at the meeting on 10 January 1963:

> Mr Stannah said that payment should be regulated in the bank credit system and the Main Contractor would not be able to withhold and use sub-contractors' money, but there was strong objection to this system from building contractors.

At the meeting on 14 October 1966:

> Mr Stannah requested that in cases where one section of a building was completed and retention money was withheld, sometimes for periods of 3 or 4 years until the whole building was completed, such retention money should be released as and when the completed part of a building was put in to commission. It was pointed out that the architect already had discretion to allow this release but it could not be enforced.

At the meeting on 13 April 1967:

> Mr Stannah referred to a recent case where the main contractor sought to impose a share of the total cost of site telephone to be paid for by subcontractors. It was recommended that such imposts should be strongly resisted.

At the meeting on 10 July 1969:

> Mr Stannah enquired if the British Standard (B.S. 2655) would ban the use of sprinkler valves in lift shafts.

At the meeting on 7 January 1971:

> Mr Stannah referred to the Secretary's circular of 7 December and the paper submitted by FASS (Federation of Associations of Specialist Subcontractors) to the Joint Contracts Tribunal relating to Clause 25 of the Standard Form of Contract. He suggested that NALM might write into its own terms of contract provision for payment by the Architect or owner in the case of default on the part of the Contractor arising from bankruptcy.

At the meeting on 13 January 1972:

> Mr Stannah commented on the circular dated 26 October in respect of plastic guide shoe linings; he advised that his company had experienced difficulties with a particular supplier due to a wide variation on tolerances; he warned members to take care when dealing with this supplier.

At the meeting on 13 April 1972:

> Mr Stannah enquired if it was possible for members to receive more information from BSI (British Standards Institute) circulars and in particular where draft specifications were concerned. The Chairman commented that members were very aware of the problems Mr Stannah had experienced on a previous occasion and believed that the Technical Committee would make every endeavour to ensure that all matters of possible interest to members were reported back to council.

SIGNIFICANT MILESTONES IN THE 1960s

Three key events occurred in the second half of the 1960s, and their influence on the subsequent evolution of the business was very significant. The first and most important was that fundamental decision in 1960 to safeguard the company assets and the future of the business with the formation on 20 March 1961 of Stannah Lifts Services Limited (Company Registration No. 686996, now styled Stannah

Lifts Holdings Limited after various name changes). This was followed by extending the geographic coverage of the service network through fortuitous acquisition opportunities which arose and were seized, leading to a substantially increased maintenance and repair portfolio and a useful product extension into lifts for seagoing vessels.

Shortly afterwards there was the decision to investigate and adopt imported components and products from Italy, leading to a wider and more standardised product range supported by Stannah's first efforts in marketing.

SPREADING OUR WINGS ON LAND AND SEA

Alan recalls that in the late 1960s two new ventures came the company's way entirely by chance, both of which changed its fortunes for the better.

> During conversation with the then Secretary of The National Association of Lift Makers, Pop learned that a small Eastbourne based lift company, Southern Lifts Ltd, had encountered financial difficulties and had been placed in Receivership – the Receiver needing another company to assume responsibility for completing unfinished work, so that he could collect monies owing in respect of the value of the work done to-date.

Brian continues:

> The Receiver, whom Pop and I visited in Eastbourne, was a local Accountant. I remember his rather quaint office and his filing system. His desk was a dining table in the centre of the room with about a dozen dining chairs set around the walls. These were not for seating, but were occupied by his work-in-progress – one file per chair and in order of priority. As one case file was closed, a Secretary solemnly removed it, then moved every file along to its neighbouring chair and a new file introduced as tail-end-Charlie.
>
> Our visit resulted in our acquisition of the assets of the business for a fairly nominal value paid for the service contracts plus our willingness to complete the outstanding orders for lifts, I believe, at cost. In fact, no cash passed at the time – we paid for the service business from the quarterly receipts. The benefits gained, were additions to our service portfolio; the goodwill of existing customers and Kent and Sussex Architects and Builders (there being much construction of retirement flats along the coast at that time); and our first out-of-London office (with clerical and technical staff). But that wasn't all.

When Stannah acquired Southern Lifts in Eastbourne in the late 1960s they inherited a contract to install a ten-stop (ten-deck) lift in an 80,000-ton oil-tanker (the *Marquina*) to be built at El Ferrol in Spain. Subsequently, Brian cut his teeth on shipyard work during the installation, which was mainly carried out by shipyard workers with no lift knowledge. While the installation progressed, the ship was moved during the fit-out programme to Cartagena and Cadiz. This was, perhaps, Brian's first experience of supervision, certainly in a foreign language. Here are a couple of his memories.

Whilst at Cartagena, I decided to visit Gibraltar – at that time, virtually impossible due to Spain's claim to sovereignty. I recall entering a house by its front door in Spain and, via the back door, arriving in Gibraltar. Everything was painted red, white and blue.

He had a miraculous escape on one of his trips to Spain. He recalls:

To-ing and fro-ing to the Spanish yards, I regularly flew Iberia in and out of Madrid. Returning to London one day I missed the Caravelle I was booked on. Just as well – it crashed. By an amazing coincidence, Alan's parents-in-law, Tom and Connie Harrison, were booked on that same Caravelle flight but were given a lift to the airport and caught an earlier plane. By such chance happenings, our lives are changed. (Earlier, in December 1957, Pop and I ran for our train home at London Bridge and it pulled out just as we got on the platform. Again, just as well. The St John's rail crash was headline news next morning, 90 people lost their lives. The disaster happened in thick fog when a train went through a red signal and ran into the back of another stationary engine between St John's and Lewisham stations. The impact itself was devastating, but then the derailed carriages knocked out bridge supports and tons of metal and concrete entombed passengers in the wreckage below. A further tragedy was narrowly averted when a following train was brought to a halt just yards from the carnage after the crash.)

Another opportunity arose soon afterwards when the Stannahs heard that the London Lift Company had also hit difficulties. With their Southern Lifts experience fresh in their minds, they concluded an identical 'takeover', bringing further additions to their service portfolio and new customers and contacts, together with contracts to be fulfilled and completed. One such (and what a coincidence) was the installation of a passenger lift in a new cross-channel ferry being built in Holland for the ferry company, Townsend (later to become Townsend Thoresen and then part of P&O). More valuable experience and minimal cost.

THE ITALIAN CONNECTION

In the late 1960s Brian and Alan were looking at ways of reducing the company's reliance on 'bespoke', which inevitably meant 'one-off', lifts. They gradually changed the company from a machine shop with lathes, milling machines, boring machines, shaping machines and planing machines to one whereby they became steel fabricators and bought in the proprietary parts of their lifts. At this time they bought their first guillotine and bending machine, the need for standardised design and manufacture having become clear. The first sheet metal bending machine was

4.9 Alan Stannah in his 505 racing dinghy designed by John Westell.

manually operated and the first Rushworth powered guillotine was far from new, but it was a major step forward at the time.

Alan Stannah recalls what followed and how events arose:

With my background of control system design, I decided to try my hand at selling lift control panels around the trade. I don't believe I sold a single one, but it did lead to a tip from one of our competitors that changed our future.

Meeting with Mr Palmer of Porn and Dunwoody Lifts Limited and trying to sell him my control panels, we fell to discussing other difficulties of our business. At that time we made our own brakes and winding gears by machining in our workshop a collection of grey iron castings which were frequently misshapen or suffered from

121

blow-holes or other imperfections. On hearing of this, Palmer laughed and said he had solved that problem – he bought them in from Germany.

I recounted this tale to Brian, who said he'd had a salesman in the office a few months previously trying to sell him their winding gears. At that time he wasn't interested and he had thrown away their catalogue. However, he recalled that in throwing it he had missed the wastepaper basket and it had fallen behind a bookcase. We pulled this from the wall and rescued the catalogue. I made contact with the company, Faer, in Rome and made my first overseas business trip – at the colossal cost then of a £70 air fare [about £1,100 today]. I had a very short haircut before I left, wishing to impress them as a smart businessman and was met in Rome by Bruno Svorazzini who had long curling locks. We went to their factory and I saw an old man who I took to be the labourer. It turned out he was Mr Svorazzini Senior, a brilliant engineer who had designed the machine tools upon which their winding gears were made – ensuring good quality and competitive prices. Bruno was good company and showed me the sights of Rome that evening, including the Coliseum and the wolves that were kept there. No doubt owing to too much Italian red wine and Grappa, Bruno persuaded me we had to howl to the wolves under the Roman full moon. I don't recall whether they howled back, but it was a great evening and the start of a business relationship that lasted for many years.

Alan Stannah also recalls:

Adopting the Faer winding gears was a turning point in our fortunes, as it simplified our production and pointed the way to the future.

I wondered then whether I could repeat the experience, so I wrote to lift companies around the world – USA, Japan, Italy – and I received many replies. However, it stood out that the Italian lift component industry was head and shoulders above the rest and it was to these companies that I wrote and made arrangements to visit and inspect their equipment.

One of the companies I had written to, Paravia in Salerno, and whom I planned to visit, had passed my enquiry on to the Daldoss company in Trento, who wrote to us giving details of their packaged service lifts. Brian and I discussed this, but owing to our unsatisfactory experience with service lifts we consigned the letter to the waste paper bin.

One of their claims was installation could be achieved by one man in one day.

As I left the office that evening, I said to Brian, 'You know there might be something in these service lifts' and I took the letter from the wastepaper bin and wrote to Daldoss asking for more details. They promised to supply their lifts in a few cardboard boxes and confirmed that we could install in a day. (They had apparently made this offer to a competitor who had laughed and said their fitters did not open their toolboxes on the first day, hence the opportunity came to us.) We said we would be happy to give it a try. We sold a couple of lifts to a hotel in Brighton and Guido Cestari came over from Italy and installed them both in two days. We were con-

The **microlift** *electronic* ®
is specially designed for use in
Hotels, Restaurants, Bars, Hospitals
Private homes, etc.
Attractive design together with
quiet operation permits use in
public areas.

Cleanliness is assured with
stainless steel or durable baked
enamel finishes.

Technical details
of the **microlift** *electronic* ®

2 Load capacities - 112 lb and 224 lb
3 Car sizes - small, medium and large
Entrances on up to 3 sides
Service at 2 to 10 floors
Low headroom at top floor - 8' - 10½'
Indicators - Lift Moving and Lift Here
Electronic control gives
Reliability and ease of servicing
Delivery - Normally ex-stock
Installation - A few days
Builders work - Easy to arrange
                    With our simple drawings.

4.10 The Daldoss company in Trento, Italy, wrote to Stannah about their packaged service lifts, which they claimed could be installed in one day.

vinced and having been granted the exclusive UK Distributorship made our first foray into media advertising using an old school friend, David Ling, as our advertising agent with the slogan 'Straight Up Sir'. From this small beginning our Microlift company and our longstanding association with what became Daldoss Elevetronic Spa was formed and it is still an important part of our company today.

Our previous experience with service lifts derived from those supplied to the GPO (General Post Office) and, more recently, in significant numbers to J. Sainsbury who, at that time, were changing the face of their previously old fashioned stores with the introduction of the new self-service concept. [Brian recalls shopping at the West Wickham branch in the late 1940s, where the process involved visits to the various counters where cheese and butter, bacon, dry goods, biscuits, etc., were individually dispensed. It was necessary to queue at each to be served, whereupon the bill for each element of the weekly shop had to be paid, with the cash conveyed by overhead wire to the High Priestess who controlled the master till, returning change and receipt in the same way to the assistants serving the shoppers. A tedious process and one the self-service model superseded.] The company made many 'tray lifts' for Sainsbury, a small self-supported service lift of about 100 weight (circa 50 kg) capacity. They were fairly agricultural in the way they were made, costly to produce and not very profitable. Installation typically involving lift erector (as they were then known) and mate for two weeks, over 20 man days.

The introduction of the Microlift thus transformed this part of our business.

Alan continues:

At that time I had just bought my first new car, a bright orange MGB GT and Jackie and I had two most interesting trips around Italy as far east as Trieste and as far south as Salerno meeting lift component suppliers, and we are still dealing with a number of these companies after approaching 40 years.

For the first of my Italian trips together with Jackie we put the MG on the train to Milan and then headed off to meet Corrado Daldoss in Trento. Corrado Daldoss had formed his company making irons and cement mixers literally by the side of the road in Trento amidst the ruins of the war. He invented the compact Microlift service lift design and was given the prize for inventors at the 1958 Brussels Exposition which got his company off to a very good start. We were very pleased to be offered the opportunity to represent his company in the UK. From Trento we travelled to Trieste in an unsuccessful attempt to sell lifts in some ships before visiting other potential suppliers in Parma and Bologna and then the long trek south down the Autostrada del Sol to Salerno. Arriving in Salerno late we wound our way along the Amalfi Drive for mile after mile with a sheer cliff on one side and a sheer drop to the Bay of Naples on the other – spectacular scenery and interesting driving. Within a mile of the hotel in Priano, the road was closed with a landslide so we wound our way back along the Amalfi Drive again to meet the Paravia family for a meal in Salerno. They then took us out to a Nightclub which, surprise, surprise, was back down the Amalfi Drive, only this time with two hot blooded Paravia brothers driving Mini Coopers racing each other flat out around the blind corners in the dark, turning their headlamps off to detect oncoming traffic when they thought it would be safe for them to drive neck and neck side by side – a truly terrifying experience.

4.11 Stannah sold a couple of Microlifts to a hotel in Brighton and Guido Cestari came over and fitted them both in two days.

4.12 Duncan LeFeuvre, apprenticed to Stannah in 1969, built up the Microlifts Division and eventually became its Managing Director.

In the end, the inevitable happened, there was a colossal pile-up, but fortunately no one was injured but Jackie was badly shaken.

So with their tail between their legs, they drove us back along the Amalfi Drive again, which made it four times that day for us. Next day the road to Priano was open. We never did any business with the Paravia brothers, but we owe them a big thank you for their introduction to Daldoss.

This was only the start of the Italian connection, which was to develop further.

As we have seen, the first two links in this chain were finding the gear manufacturing company Faer, thus replacing our handmade one-at-a-time gearboxes and brakes with their production-run geared motors which was followed by our introduction to the Daldoss Elevetronic Microlift and our receipt of the grant of the Distributorship of the product. Our minds were now opened to wider horizons and a further step was the concept and subsequent development of the Maxilift standard range of passenger lifts.

4.13 L to R: Duncan LeFeuvre, Alan Stannah, Carlo Daldoss, Luca Daldoss, Brian Stannah.

Maxilift was a happy thought embodying standardised designs; compact dimensions as a USP [unique selling point] incorporating components sourced at reduced cost with dependable quality resulting from volume production; a brand name with appealing connotations inspired by Microlift; and finally its fit with our toe-in-the-water approach to marketing.

John Bovis and Alan Stannah developed the Maxilift range together, Bovis introducing the unique feature of omitting the diverter sheave, allowing a significant reduction in headroom. These first Maxilifts incorporated a number of other unique design features. They were carefully aimed at a gap in the market and were very well received.

Thus by the end of the 1960s the company was in a shape and condition very different to that which had prevailed ten years earlier, with new service businesses extending into the south-east of England, new products based on new technology, and the experience of negotiating and executing contracts in mainland Europe.

Pete Lockton, who had joined the company as an apprentice in 1958, recalls his varied experiences:

During the late 60s and early 70s, I was working at a hospital in Sundridge Park, which entailed a very late evening to get the work finished. The 'old man' brought

4.14 John Bovis and Alan Stannah developed the Maxilift range together.

flasks of tea and cakes for us and when the job was finished about 21.30 that night came back to drive us all to the rail station.

1969 was the year of the first marine lifts to be made and installed by Stannah and when it was shipped to Holland we were all – EVERYONE on the company – taken round the pub to give it a send off.

Shortly afterwards, Lockton travelled to Holland to supervise installation.

On arrival in Holland on that 1st marine lift I was made to wait a full week before the container was allowed to be opened. On return home after completion I reported this fact to Mr Stannah who stated that he would seek compensation via the International Court. For well over a year every time I saw the 'old man' he would tell me the case was proceeding well and one day out of the blue he told me how the case had been won and that there was a little extra in my pay packet to make up for the lost bonus of that week.

Pete Lockton also recalls another example of Pop's kindness towards his employees:

An apprentice working with me had tried to either get extra pay or leave the company, due to his circumstances of being married with a young baby and having to live in rented accommodation. The 'old man' refused the pay rise so the apprentice left and was employed illegally by another company as a fitter. When Mr Stannah found out he told the larger lift company what the situation was and the apprentice was made to return to us. Questioned by Mr Stannah as to his needs and spending habits, he thought no more of it for a while until his wife told him that Mr Stannah had been round to the flat, measured it, then forced his landlord to reduce the rent in compliance with some regulations regarding size. [As related to Pete Lockton at the time by George Krise, the apprentice in question.]

Lockton also told *Elevation* in 2004 of his experiences when working on one of the ships where he was servicing the lift:

> During my many excursions abroad for Stannah's Marine division I have encountered some pretty unusual happenings, one of which occurred in Holland in 1969–70. Now for those that don't know, the purchasers of ships usually send out a special crew to oversee all the work and to learn where the pointed end is etc.
>
> Townsend, the purchasers of the 'Free Enterprise' group of ships being built by Werf Gusto of Rotterdam, were no exception, and the crew sent out all wore the usual merchant garb, which consisted of peaked cap, white overalls on top of a roll-necked sweater, with a pocket stuffed with gloves, torch etc.
>
> Derek Young was their chief electrical engineer, and a very useful person to know, helpful to lost lift men and able to communicate in Dutch with the builders, so I felt it was him I needed to see on one occasion when things were not going according to plan. However, how to find him on such a large vessel? 'I know', I thought, 'draw a picture of him and the Dutch workers will recognise him, leading me to him and therefore my salvation.'
>
> So on to the red leaded bulkhead with a piece of chalk I drew a face in profile with a peaked cap and roll-necked sweater. Calling two Dutch workers over to my 'masterpiece', I pointed to it, then to my chest, shrugged my shoulders and tried to make a face like a lost sheep, hoping this would have the desired effect.
>
> The two stood for a few minutes and were joined by some more. Then others came pushing me to the back, no word being spoken other than some muttering which I did not understand. Some more time passed and I was beginning to feel a little unsure of my tactics when all of a sudden one of this by now very large group exclaimed in a loud voice, 'AH! DE GAULLE', at which point I slipped silently away, while a loud heated discussion raged behind me over French politics.

When Lockton completed his apprenticeship in 1963, by this time working for Stannah Lift Services Limited but still at 49–51 Tiverton Street, Leslie Stannah wrote to him as follows:

> Dear Lockton,
>
> I enclose herewith your indentures duly completed on the termination of your apprenticeship and congratulate you on so doing.
>
> As you know, wherever possible it is our policy to endeavour to promote from within our own organisation and we hope, in due course, circumstances will permit us to consider you in this aspect.
>
> As I told you, when I saw you, you and your assistant may be the only members of the organisation that the customer sees and they will judge us by the way in which you conduct our affairs, control your assistant, carry out your work and start and

4.15 A ten-inch Stannah lift-winding machine of the 1960s.

finish to time. This latter I regard of the greatest importance and it is something on which I have more complaints from customers than anything else.

With best wishes

Yours sincerely,
Leslie Stannah
Managing Director

Note the 'Dear Lockton' – no 'Mr' or 'Peter'.

Peter Lockton finally retired in March 2004 after 46 years of service, having held the position of Training and Technical Systems Engineer of Stannah Lifts Limited and contributed a great deal to the success of the company.

WORKSHOP AND OFFICE EFFICIENCY

Brian Stannah himself was something of an entrepreneur (at school he had traded Hungarian hog-skin gloves from the Army and Navy Stores), and during the 1960s he built up a business making and distributing swimming pool equipment. By the late 1960s he was investing in plastic moulding machinery and moved the business into a 17,000-square-foot warehouse. It was the UK market leader in swimming pool equipment when he eventually sold the business to a management buyout in 1972. Still named Certikin, it is today a major European manufacturer of swimming pool equipment.

As always, Brian was highly organised and had taken the trouble to write out in longhand the procedures to be followed at Certikin:

Workshop management

The premises are rented partly as a favour. The landlord – J.P. Simmonds of 20 Queens Road – is himself a tenant and we therefore have a dual responsibility for safety, cleanliness and consideration for others. No nuisance must ever be caused and the fire risk must always be remembered and guarded against ... Floors will be swept daily when work is in progress. The premises will be thoroughly tidied as a last job each week. Tools will be returned to their correct places after use. Materials will be kept in a state of order. Floor space will be used as economically as possible. The premises will be locked whenever unattended. The adjoining tenant may be diplomatically approached as he may be prepared to accept deliveries in the absence of our personnel.

Inter alia, Brian said under the heading of 'Office Management':

A large diary should be maintained recording briefly all phone calls, any promises given or received with regard to deliveries etc., visits made or received, appointments etc. This can often provide useful ammunition in an argument over a past event and also act as a reminder as to when deliveries are due to be made or received.

There then follow several pages covering:

Procedure upon receipt of customer order
Purchasing Procedure
Ordering Procedure
Progressing the Order
Receipt of Goods ordered

Under the heading of 'Workshop Efficiency', Brian wrote:

The workshop is only one department of several where it must be remembered that the prime object in production is profit. A company cannot continue functioning if it is not working profitably. The degree of profit achieved per job is affected by the efficiency with which that job is executed. Efficiency really means lack of waste. Waste can occur in the use of labour, materials or in overhead costs such as heat, light, rent etc.

On 'Labour Waste' he said:

> Firstly hours worked must be 100% or above of hours paid. The word 'above' in the last sentence should not be misconstrued. The policy of this company is to recognise the efforts of staff and workers. Employees will benefit by successful growth. Growth is not possible without profits to finance that growth.
>
> Secondly hours worked must be used efficiently. Any operator should always practice a simple form of work study … Each operation and job should be the subject of a little thought and planning as to the best and most efficient way to tackle it. A golden rule, rather hackneyed but still invaluable, is 'Measure twice and cut once'. [This was advice frequently rendered by Pop Stannah.]

Under 'Material Wastage' he wrote:

> Material purchased should be sold again. Any material purchased but not used is money thrown away. Scrap should be carefully checked to make sure it really is scrap. Scrap has value. Can it be sold?

On 'Wastage of Overheads' he said:

> Lighting and heating needlessly used, power tools left running, vehicles being driven too hard, overlong telephone calls, breakage of tools and plant etc. all means waste, in effect a reduction in the ultimate profit.

There was more, on:

> Office Efficiency
> Company Accounts
> Financial Accounts
> Suggested Commission/Bonus Payment Scheme

This venture gave Brian valuable experience. Certikin, having been developed into a very successful business, was sold, Brian having decided to focus his energies on the lift business.

The Stannah Lifts company was now on a firm financial footing, thanks to the first stages of what has become a key element in the Stannah business philosophy – that the company should achieve strength and stability through standing on many legs. The legs that had now been established were a growing service and repair business in London and the south-east, a standardised range of Maxilift passenger lifts based on a carefully structured balance between manufactured and bought-in proprietary components, and the growing Microlift goods-only lift business.

During the 1960s, the Tiverton Street premises had evolved since they were rebuilt in 1947. Pop bought the adjoining site, the cottages thereon having suffered

4.16, 4.17 The 1960s, often looked on as a decade of liberation, was not an easy decade in which to build a business. First, there was the US involvement in Vietnam. Secondly, there was violence in Northern Ireland.

4.18 At least England won the football World Cup, Bobby Moore captaining the team to an exciting victory over the old enemy, Germany, in 1966.

the same fate as A.J'.s factory – the chance target of a German bomb. Pop subsequently designed a more permanent replacement for the Nissen hut, to be built in stages – single-storey at first but with provision for a further storey, the floor of which had a removable section to facilitate the assembly of unusually high lift cars. Both stages were completed a few years apart, both on a shoestring and using the company's resources as much as possible.

Brian recalls:

> The first stage had pitched roof lights along each side supported by an upstand on the reinforced concrete ceiling which would double eventually as the slab for the first floor planned to follow. When we started the second phase, I remember working with Norman Anderson building the walls of the upper floor in block work. Saturdays and Sundays were not sacrosanct in those days.

GROWING FINANCIAL STABILITY

The first year of the new company, Stannah Lift Services Ltd returned a respectable trading profit of £3,779.4.11 on sales of £35,833.7.3 (in today's money these numbers would be £75,000 profit on sales of £720,000). Mind you, costs were being kept rigidly under control. Labour charges were:

Shop foreman   £825.7.11
Labour   £2,878.10.4
Erection Supervisor   £909.5.0
Outside Labour   £7,985.18.0
Drawing Office expenses and salaries   £1,469.19.6
Salaries   £856.3.8

Total bank charges were only £71.17.10, although this was without taking into account the bank loan taken out by Leslie Stannah secured against the Tiverton Street premises which provided the essential working capital. Alan recalls this was in the order of £12,000, which represented a massive financial mountain to climb. It was only in the late 1960s with the improved earnings and cash-flow arising from the company's expanded service portfolio that this debt was cleared and the threat of the bailiffs at the door was at last put behind them.

In the following year to 31 December 1963, sales were slightly down at £33,188.18.1 with gross profit at £10,307.15.2, slightly higher than the £10,091 of the previous year. However, trading profit fell sharply to only £1,520.13.2. This seemed to be due to increased salary and wage costs in all areas. At least the company was able to pay back Leslie Stannah over £3,000 of his loan.

By the mid-1960s the British economy was struggling, especially in comparison with its overseas rivals – although, looking back from the early 21st century, the growth rates achieved appear quite respectable. But sterling was clearly overvalued and the Labour government under Harold Wilson, elected in October 1964 after thirteen years of Conservative rule, refused to contemplate devaluation even though many leading economists and many in the City favoured it and, indeed, saw it as inevitable. The government preferred controls and interference and introduced the Prices and Incomes Act in August 1966, part of a package of measures designed to improve the balance of payments and shore up sterling following a seamen's strike in the early summer.

At Stannah, 1964 brought a 25 per cent rise in sales to nearly £45,000, a 60 per cent rise in gross profits to nearly £20,000 and a 350 per cent rise in trading profit to nearly £7,500. 1965 brought further progress, with sales rising to £50,000, although gross profits slipped back to £18,500 and trading profit fell 40 per cent to £4,470.

In 1966, the year of England's World Cup triumph but also, more important to most businesses, the year of a dock strike and of a crisis, deflationary budget in July, Stannah managed a slight increase in sales to £52,500, a reasonable increase in gross profits to £21,000 and a 34 per cent increase in trading profit to £6,000.

People may wonder how two brothers have managed to work so closely together to build a successful business. This is how Brian Stannah explains it:

> From the earliest days at Tiverton Street in London, we've always shared an office whilst principally focusing on different responsibilities. The advantage of sharing an office is that we've always had an ear open for what the other was doing and able to chip in with helpful or irritating comments.
>
> Development of ideas has followed on similar lines, rather like ping pong balls being batted to and fro. Whilst we both served engineering apprenticeships and thus have technical backgrounds, Alan moved naturally towards design, product innovation and manufacturing control, with an electrical bias, whereas I tended towards the more commercial side of the business, sales, service operations and accounts – and that's pretty much the way it has stayed.
>
> Our most valuable asset is our team of loyal staff without whom we wouldn't have a successful business. We enjoy an easy relationship with them. They are on first name terms with me and Alan – I can't say the reverse is always true with so many faces to recognise. It wasn't always so. When we joined Pop the done thing was for the sons to be addressed as Mr Brian and Mr Alan and one or two old hands still do it. [I think you will recall that Alan Godley had abbreviated it to 'Mr A.' – that's always how he addressed or referred to Alan.] Quite a contrast with the greater formality in Germany, where Herr Wolfgang Seick, the owner and Managing Director of our German distributor, Hopmann, at the time, would always shake everyone by the hand coming into the office in the morning and address them formally. I have noticed that that continues to this day, where his son Harald continues the convention. When we first moved from London to Andover and subsequently had our first office built alongside the factory we had it designed such that all personnel entered by the same door – another important little bit of philosophy. We'd do the same today if numbers permitted.

In spite of the generally difficult economic environment the company achieved a great leap forward in 1967, with sales jumping by 41 per cent to £74,200. Gross profits increased by an even greater 63 per cent to £34,260 and trading profits by an impressive 135 per cent to £14,100.

1968, the first year of trading after the pound sterling's notorious devaluation from $2.80 to $2.40 to the pound in November 1967, brought the milestone of the company's turnover reaching £100,000 (about £2 million in today's money). This meant it had grown 100 per cent in less than three years. Gross profits moved up in line but trading profit, at £15,429, was only 9 per cent ahead.

Stannah recruited Len Rogers, who had been a sales manager with the Glasgow lift manufacturer, A. and P. Stevens, where, you will remember, Pop Stannah had worked for a short time in the 1930s. Pop thought he would bring extra sales expertise to the company and a maturity that would be helpful to the young Brian and Alan, although, in the event, Brian was not happy with the situation. Brian Stannah said later of Len Rogers:

> We needed more sales resource and Len Rogers was available. To attract him, Pop offered him a Directorship. This made him a somewhat uncomfortable bed fellow. We should have employed him as a salesman, which he was – and a good one. Maybe the Director title helped open doors but it was a mistake.

Alan Mott was the company accountant who previously at John King and Partners had carried out the audit. He left in the early 1970s and was replaced by Colin Waas, a Sri Lankan. Brian Stannah said later:

> Waas contributed much to our systems, installing formal budgetary control for the first time. He and I together made the case to Test Valley in our application for relocation to Andover (see below). That wasn't a pushover and we had to work hard to convince them that we were worthy as a prospective lessee on their new Portway Industrial Estate.

Building on previous experience with marine lifts, Brian, being the sales and marketing (such as it was) brother, started to promote the new-found expertise and further marine lifts followed – first for Townsend (became Townsend Thoresen later) in Holland and Denmark. Then lines of bulk carriers, first in Brazil at a part-Dutch, part-Brazilian joint venture, Verolme, then in Canada at Marine Industries Limited at Montreal, Province of Quebec. He observed:

> Then at last a contract was won for a ship to be built at a British yard. This was for the first of the new line of Type 42 Destroyers, the lifts being required to keep the Captain and his Bridge party refuelled with food and drink. The lifts were required to operate under conditions of 30 degrees roll and 15 degrees pitch whilst all guns were firing. It would have required nerves of steel to enjoy sustenance under such

conditions. As I recall Vickers Barrow were the lead design yard and it was to them that my first visit was paid after receipt of the order. There I learnt that because the MOD had set a policy of identicality, we were to automatically receive the orders for another nine or ten lifts, one in each of the forthcoming Type 42s to be built in various yards including Camel Laird and Swanhunter (our first introduction to Tyneside). Not long into the series we became concerned that costs were higher than expected owing to the stringent demands of the MOD and the associated procedures. Amazingly we succeeded in renegotiating the contract price per lift based (would you believe it) on the thickness of the file containing the paperwork for the first contract compared with that of a typical commercial contract – the one in question being that of the Sheineman family referred to earlier. Eventually when the shipbuilding boom died or rather shifted to Japan, the run of Type 42s came to an end and that was the end of our marine exploits, at least until we became involved with the Jubilee Sailing Trust years later.

By the early 1970s Stannah had progressed dramatically in its method of manufacturing from the days of the early 1960s, described here by Alan Stannah:

4.19 (above) *In the 1970s, Stannah won a contract to install lifts in the new Type 42 Destroyers for the Royal Navy, including* HMS Sheffield *(shown here) which was eventually sunk by an Exocet missile in the Falklands War of 1982.*
4.20 (left) *Stannah also installed lifts into passenger ships.*

In Stannah Lifts we have adapted our manufacturing to many changes over the years. When I joined the company in the early 1960s our manufacturing was largely machining grey iron castings and other materials to make gearboxes, brakes, door locks, driving and diverter sheaves and other components for our range of passenger lifts. All these were made in small numbers which was rapidly becoming uneconomical. We found we could better source these from outside suppliers (mainly from Italy) and we accordingly re-allocated our manufacturing, first to steel fabrication using rolled steel channels and joists, and then to sheet metal fabrication for our lift cars and doors, and later for stairlift manufacture.

These changes from our older production methods were a very traumatic transition for Pop, who was deeply attached to a roomful of pine patterns and core boxes for a multitude of cast lift components representing a very substantial capital investment. The problems were that it was no longer economical to make these components in the small numbers we required as the machining was very labour intensive and also by then we were beginning to expand and desperately needed the space. It was my job to arrange for these to be put to the torch and it took a long time for Pop to forgive me for this.

In 1972 Stannah broke through not only £200,000 in turnover but £300,000 as well, finishing at £309,452. Sales had been only £52,500 in 1966. Gross profit had also nearly reached £100,000, though trading profit was still only £19,800.

And this was achieved in spite of a troubled economic and political background which, as we shall see, proved to be a blessing in disguise.

The most severe defeat experienced by the government came in early 1972 when it caved in to the miners. Furthermore, the flying pickets organised by a new-style miners' leader from Yorkshire, Arthur Scargill, made both the government and the police look clumsy. On 9 January 1972 a national coal strike began, the first since 1926, after the union had rejected the employers' offer of an 8 per cent wage increase. After successful picketing of many key coal depots and power stations, the government appointed a Committee of Inquiry under a High Court judge, Lord Wilberforce. Already known for having given the power workers a 20 per cent increase the year before, Wilberforce soon recommended a very large increase for the miners. However, the National Union of Mineworkers (NUM) rejected this offer by 23 votes to two. After further negotiations and concessions, the miners won a total earnings increase of between 17 and 24 per cent and the strike was eventually called off on 21 February. The Economist, which had encouraged the Coal Board and government to take a tough line, saying: 'The miners cannot stop the country in its tracks as they once could have done', was seen as too optimistic. The miners seemed to have come pretty close to halting the country.

By the end of 1972 the loosening of credit controls by the Chancellor, Anthony, now Lord, Barber, had created boom conditions in the British economy, and for much of 1973 the problem for manufacturers was not the level of orders but of securing supplies and at the right cost. After the pause in 1971 the world economy was also growing strongly. As we shall see, this burst of growth was to prove very short-lived but, for the moment, the manufacturers' task was to take full advantage.

1973 brought yet another substantial jump in turnover to almost £400,000 and this time an equally sharp jump in trading profit to £33,685.

During the Barber boom of 1972–73 work was plentiful and at good prices. This was followed by the inevitable downturn, as can be seen from the table (right) which shows the lift industry statistics for Stannah Lifts' traction passenger lift market from 1971 through to 1980.

It is said that when the going gets tough, the tough get going – and Stannah's response to these difficult times brought the greatest change in the company's history, which will unfold in the following chapters.

Year	Number of traction lifts sold in the industry
1971	3,265
1972	3,399
1973	3,443
1974	2,520
1975	1,575
1976	1,591
1977	1,228
1978	1,337
1979	1,424
1980	1,233

4.21 Staff at Tiverton Street.

CHAPTER FIVE

1973–1985

READY FOR TAKE-OFF

MORE ABOUT MICROLIFTS

In 1969, Stannah had employed a bright young apprentice, Duncan LeFeuvre. When they needed someone to take responsibility for the Microlift business, they gave this opportunity to Duncan, who grasped it with both hands. LeFeuvre set

141

5.1 Alan Stannah and Duncan LeFeuvre on a visit to Daldoss in Italy.

himself up in premises, formerly a retail shop in Lodge Road, Southampton. He took on the responsibility of sales and was assisted by Rod Metcalfe as installer and Jill Aldridge to handle the administration. Their main sales target was the architectural profession. Architects were the people who specified in their drawings for pubs, restaurants and hotels that they should have a service lift, and LeFeuvre wanted to make sure they specified a Stannah Microlift.

The little team was successful enough to prompt a move, first to bigger premises in Renown Close, Chandlers Ford, and then sharing a building on the Portway Industrial Estate, Andover with Stannah Lifts Domestic Products, as the Stairlifts company was originally called.

A very close relationship with the Daldoss company and the Daldoss family developed. Corrado had two sons, Luca and Carlo. Luca came to England to improve his English, to be followed more recently by his daughter, Caterina, and Carlo's son, Carlo Alberto, who both worked with the Stannah companies in Andover. These contacts established firm friendships which have lasted to this day.

Dickie Staff, who joined Stannah as an apprentice in 1976 and fulfilled a number of roles in Stannah Microlifts Limited, finally holding the position of Safety and Quality Manager, recalled that Stannah grew to be Daldoss's largest customer, taking nearly 1,000 lifts a year, about a third of the Italian company's production.

The first Microlifts offered load capacities of 50kg and 100kg, but it was soon obvious that there was a market for goods-only lifts with a larger load capacity. The first such lift to be developed in conjunction with the Daldoss company was the Trolleylift, with a load capacity of 250kg. Such was its success that in the 1980s Stannah Microlifts Limited introduced a new product which they called the Loadmaster, a lift made by a family company, Schönau, based in Hamburg. However, they were unable to establish a similar relationship to the one they enjoyed with Daldoss, whom they then asked to develop a similar product to Loadmaster. This product, called Goodsmaster, was eventually introduced to the market and has proved to be a valuable addition to the Microlifts product range.

And who were the customers? According to Dickie:

Many service lifts are installed in catering environments, one of our most famous customers being Luigi Primavera and his restaurant in Covent Garden. Luigi was one of Duncan's first customers some 35 years ago. His two 50kg lifts were installed 'side by side', and have been in constant use ever since, with no major breakdown or repair needed. Last year Crayford Service Branch refurbished them and installed a further two Microlifts to cope with Luigi's increase in trade.

Other 'claims to fame' are installations at Bill Wyman's – of Rolling Stones fame – 'Sticky Fingers' restaurant in Kensington, prestige London hotels such as the Café Royal, Dorchester and Mayfair. Customers range from high street banks, building societies and travel agents, to wine merchants, off-licences and registered charity shops. We have even installed in a famous Royal couple's new house in Berkshire.

5.2, 5.3 Stannah Trolleylift and Goodsmaster. These were supplied to Richard Branson's Virgin Records headquarters, Sony Music's offices and warehouses, Lord's Cricket Ground, Arsenal Football Club and Newbury Racecourse.

Trolleylifts and Goodsmaster lifts can be found at Richard Branson's Virgin Records' headquarters, Sony Music's offices and warehouses, and at British Airways at Heathrow Airport, as well as Lord's Cricket Ground, Arsenal Football Club and Newbury Racecourse.

Alastair Stannah gives details here of typical Microlift customers in 2004:

We have maintained a steady flow of lifts for all sorts of applications, some diverse and distant, ranging from pubs (for various breweries, including Regent Inns, Mitchell's & Butler's, Pubmaster, Scottish and Newcastle, Hall & Woodhouse, Burtonwood Brewery, Punch Pub Co., Unique Pub Co., Barracuda Group, Geronimo), restaurants (Costa Coffee, Loch Fyne, Ponti's, Carluccio's), nightclubs and casinos (Luminar Leisure, Ultimate Leisure, Gala Casinos), golf and rugby clubs and indoor sports tracks (Murrayfield Indoor Sports Club), a Thames Rowing Club (Auriol & Kensington), a gentlemen's club in London (The Worshipful Company of Pewterers), hotels (Holiday Inn Express, Manor House Hotel at Castle Combe, Cricklewood Hotel), hospitals (Birmingham Children's Hospital, Goodmayes Hospital, Sheffield Northern General, Bristol BUPA Hospital), a magistrates' court, a fire brigade headquarters, shoe shops the length and breadth of the UK (Dolcis, Clarks, Aldo, Faith, Top Shop), the Diamond Trading Centre, prisons, schools, colleges and universities (Brunel University, Whitelands College, Westgate School, Winchester, Campsmount Technology College, Joseph Rowntree School in York), Twycross Zoo, high street bakeries (Greggs, Baker's Oven), plus high profile retail customers (Poundland, Argos, New Look, Habitat, Hugo Boss, KFC, Lloyds Pharmacy, Budgens, Holland & Barrett, Co-op Stores).

HOMELIFTS AND STAIRLIFTS

Stannah Lifts Limited suffered in common with others in the lift industry from the effect of a nasty combination of an oil shortage and a miners' strike on the UK and indeed the world economy at the end of 1973 and on into 1974. Construction was badly hit and the annual demand for traction passenger lifts fell from 3,443 in 1973 to 1,228 by 1977.

Stannah's product, Homelift, was born out of this recession. With the demand for commercial lifts much reduced, Alan Stannah proposed that the company make a homelift. There seemed to be a demand and Stannah had been turning prospective purchasers away. Alan Stannah remembered that he and Brian worked on in the office after the switchboard had closed and many of the phone calls were from people enquiring about homelifts.

With their existing knowledge and technology, it was a relatively simple task to design the new small lift, John Bovis readily rising to the challenge. It was based on the proven Microlift drive package, thus avoiding the need for extensive life testing. Brian began to sell the Homelift in 1974 and it quickly became apparent that there were people with a need and the money. However, in most cases, the

5.4 *The whole country suffered from economic problems in the early 1970s caused by inflation, a national miners' strike and the rocketing price of oil.*

5.5 *A Stannah Homelift. This Stannah lift was born out of the recession of 1973–5. With the demand for commercial lifts much reduced, Alan Stannah proposed that the company make a homelift.*

architecture of their homes meant they could not accommodate a lift. Brian Stannah said:

> I would walk away leaving an unsatisfied prospect and with no order for the factory. In my subconscious lurked the word stairlift, though I'd never seen one, and it occurred to me that such a product would present an alternative and give me a second string to my salesman's bow. So the recession was a disguised blessing. Without it I doubt we would be here today.

In search of a new product, Brian Stannah identified a stairlift being developed in Holland by a company called Jan Hamer run by Pieter Mulder. Shrewdly, Brian bought the drawings for a fee and a royalty for a short number of years, and Stannah began to make stairlifts. This was a far-sighted and inspired initiative that was to have a profound effect on the future growth and fortunes of the company.

Jan Hamer's stairlift had a rail custom-made for each order and incorporated bends when necessary to follow the many stairway designs.

Stairlift production began in 1975, 66 units being sold by 31 December. Sales doubled in 1976, doubled again in 1977 and yet again in 1978. Alan remembers the difficulties of the early stairlift production:

> The Tiverton Street premises were not suited to the manufacture of the curved stairlift rails, which came in a wonderful variety of shapes and sizes to suit the complexities of our customers' staircases.
>
> Initially we sought assistance from specialist steel fabricators in making the bends for us to assemble together with the intermediate straight sections of tube to produce the completed stairlift rails. This turned out to be an expensive blind alley, resulting in piles of scrap bends but little in the way of useful output. Fortunately sales were fairly slow initially, at the rate of about one per week, which gave us time to develop the necessary fabricating skills.
>
> This did prove very difficult at first. In fact, at one time we were removing them for remedial work as fast as they were being installed. This is etched in my memory as a very difficult time for us (perhaps the most stressful that I have experienced during my working life) but we battled through, improved our production methods and the rest, as they say, is history.
>
> A stumbling block in the early days of stairlift production was that the gearboxes and motors supplied by the company recommended by Jan Hamer lacked power and reliability. Our first production did not carry the designed full load. This could have stopped the project in its tracks, but fortunately in the nick of time John Bovis located a suitable unit from the Tornado company in Berlin who made a product designed for garage door operators which was found to be ideally suited for the requirements of a stairlift drive system. This was quickly adopted into our production. We found the Tornado company under the leadership of Peter Wiest was very efficient and pleasant to deal with and this relationship has continued to the present day.

By the early 1970s, with the required output nearing the limit of the London factory and creating great pressure on those working there, Alan Stannah recalled that they held many what he called 'moans' meetings when they would sit down in the evenings and listen to the complaints and suggestions for improvements. Alan says:

> We learnt a wonderful lesson through these meetings – of the commitment and interest of our work people and the value of the ideas of the people who had hands-on experience. We have continued applying the lesson we learnt then to this day.

1974 brought up the £0.5 million mark in sales, the first time the word 'million' appeared. After the inflationary years of the 1970s and 1980s we have all got used to millions, but it must have been an exciting moment in those days. Admittedly the rate of inflation had been rising quite sharply in the early 1970s, and it reached the horrendous annual rate of 26 per cent in the UK in mid-1975. Nevertheless, in absolute terms, Stannah Lift Services Limited's sales in 1974 were nearly ten times what they had been eight years earlier in 1966. Just as important, trading profit at £70,000 was a creditable 14 per cent of those sales.

RELOCATION TO ANDOVER

By 1972 the Tiverton Street premises at the Elephant and Castle were under severe stress, no longer serving the needs of the growing business and already overspilling into the nearby railway arches. When London's railways were originally constructed they were imposed on the pre-existing infrastructure, and many sections were raised to clear the road system. These raised sections were constructed in brickwork which formed columns to support the permanent way above. Much of the structure made use of arches, developed originally by the Romans as a means of bearing the distributed load, the spaces below being turned into commercial use by British Rail who rented the dark and frequently dank spaces to those in need. There was a ready supply close to Tiverton Street and these proved to offer a temporary solution to the company's needs.

However, this was the limit of what was possible with the Tiverton Street premises, which, if a solution was not found, would be a constraint on the future growth of the company.

Decisions, therefore, had to be taken. Alan and Brian started to consider possible locations ranging from the valleys of South Wales to a disused railway station at Partridge Green in Sussex, but none seemed to fit the bill. However, Alan read of the GLC Expanding Towns Scheme whereby companies were encouraged to move from London to the country at attractive ground rents and with guaranteed housing for employees. Ashford in Kent and Andover in Hampshire were possible locations, so Brian took himself down to Andover and returned full of enthusiasm for what the town had to offer – an excellent central location, with first-class road access.

After the Second World War, part of the brave new world which politicians of both left and right promised Londoners was the chance to build new lives for themselves away from the slums of inner London. As a result, not only did the outer suburbs of London itself expand, but towns further into the countryside were designated 'new' towns and were developed out of all recognition from the very small towns, or really only villages, that they had been before the war.

One such town was Andover on the River Anton in Hampshire. Andover lay just below the Harrow Way, an ancient route which crossed the south of England from western Cornwall to the North Downs of Kent near Dover. It had enabled trade in Irish gold, Cornish tin and other commodities.

By the mid-1700s Andover had become an important staging post between London and Exeter, and from 1783 this included carriage of the Royal Mail. By the end of the 18th century there were no fewer than 50 inns in the town, many of them on the new Andover turnpike and some with their own brewery. Horse-drawn coaches would give way to railways, which arrived in Andover in 1854.

Andover enjoyed and also suffered, as did other English towns, the vicissitudes down through the centuries, such as the Roman occupation and various civil wars between kings and their barons, a town fire in 1435 and a plague in 1603.

In modern times, Andover's expansion began with the Town Development Act of 1952 which, as John MacDonald wrote in his book *Around Andover*, was designed

to help overcrowded industry move out of London. London County Council's request for Andover to take industry and 6,000 people was rejected, and Hampshire County turned down a scheme for a new town at Hook. Finally Andover and Basingstoke were suggested for expansion and negotiations began.

By the autumn of 1960, a Joint Committee of three members from each authority under a chairman from the Borough was meeting regularly in the Guildhall, and the officers and consultants of all three were acting jointly in support. Compulsory purchase of farmland and property in the town centre began to get under way.

In May 1961 Andover Borough, Hampshire County Council and London County Council signed an agreement for Andover to take industry from London, and for land or industrial units to be on offer and housing to be built, and redevelopment of a central area as shops and public buildings in a new Town Centre. The furore of protest in the Drill Hall owed much of its force to protesters who had reversed fluoridation in 1957, and to others just spoiling for a fight, but the 'Advertiser' poll of public views and the Borough's pamphlet 'Heard in the High Street' showed that anti town-development had no support, and the Borough Council approved the Development Plan of the prestigious LCC Architects Department.

By 1964 houses on the first of the estates, Floral Way, were being occupied and other estates rapidly followed. The first industrial estates at Walworth and East Portway were well under way, and all seemed to be going to plan.

5.6, 5.7 Andover in rural Hampshire – Stannah moved its head office and main manufacturing plant there in 1973. It had been a country village but was now designated an expansion town.

The Andover bypass circling the south side of town was opened in 1969, assuming the identity of the A303 which in the centre of town was often congested, even if the level crossing had gone. The northern loop road, built the previous year, gave entry to the industrial estates, and once completed and connected to the bypass, made an effective ring road.

In 1972 Stannah Lifts Limited made its requirements known to Andover Borough Council, whose strategic plan of that time included provision for two major industrial areas on their Walworth and Portway estates. Land would be available on long leases of 99 years for development by both users and developers, subject to satisfying an approval process. The company accountant at that time, as we have seen, was Colin Waas, a very bright Sri Lankan who was well liked, and he and Brian combined in bringing their persuasive forces to bear upon the Andover Borough

5.8 The early factory built to Stannah's specifications.

Council. A well-thought-out and well-presented business plan was required. Waas had already improved and modernised the company's financial processes, and put effective budgetary control in place. The necessary management systems, including the espousal of 'Management by Objectives', were, therefore, available and in place to create and justify the application to the Council.

The proposal, after some fairly hard probing, was approved. Brian then selected a firm of architects, Burford and Partners of Southgate Street, Winchester, who already had clients on the East Portway Estate who were well satisfied with their work. Alan and Norman Anderson joined in to agree the brief. A lease was granted to the company which provided for sufficient land to accommodate 20,000 sq. ft. (1,871 sq. m.) of factory.

The final plan provided for a high-roof square building to be constructed in a number of stages each of 5,000 sq. ft. (468 sq. m.) with full overhead crane coverage, necessary for the efficient production methods used at the time.

While Andover was in many ways an ideal town to expand into, it had one drawback – just about the lowest unemployment rate in the country. Thus when in 1972 the decision to move was made, one of the first steps was to recruit three sixteen-year-old school-leavers as apprentices and place them in off-the-job training at the Basingstoke Technical College, timed for them to complete their course for the opening of the new factory the following year. In 2017, one of those apprentices, Paul Clifton, is a Director of Stannah Lifts Limited, and another, Steve

Clacy, is a valued and experienced member of the Stairlifts Product Development Team. Paul, his twin brother Dave and Steve all worked as the advance guard in the new factory, setting up work benches and machine tools for the opening in August 1973.

By the time the new factory opened, the business was doing well enough for the workshop in London to be retained and there was no need for any redundancies. There were plenty of volunteers for the move to Andover and the new factory was soon in regular production.

The move to Andover was going to have its exciting, and also difficult, moments. After all, not every Londoner wants to move permanently to the middle of the countryside. This is how Alan Holloway, who worked for Stannah for 25 years, remembers it:

> We were one of the first families to move from London to Andover with Stannah in 1974. I was a young married man and I relocated to Andover with my dear wife Jan. Both of us are Londoners and these were exciting times!
>
> We were one of seven families who moved to Andover in the late summer of 1974, four of which were new employees and their families. Norman Anderson had relocated to Whitchurch some months earlier. It was Norman's job to co-ordinate the building of the new factory at Watt Close together with the transfer of plant and equipment from Tiverton Street in London. I will always be thankful to Norman for his tireless efforts on our relocation and for ensuring that we were allocated a new house.
>
> Here I was, a newly married man with a new job, new house and a new place of work. We didn't find it easy and it was a little while before we settled into the area, but Jan and I had the support of the other families who had relocated to Andover together with the unfailing support of the company.
>
> During the following months a second group of families arrived from London and manufacturing commenced in earnest. The first phase of the factory dwarfed the manufacturing area in London. The plot of ground around the factory was so big we were given permission to develop small allotments where we grew vegetables (rabbits permitting).
>
> As the years went on we saw the introduction of new products and we just grew and grew. The second, third and fourth phase of the factory was built together with the offices as you see them today. I don't know how to explain it but although the company grew literally month on month with many new people joining I still felt the same exciting buzz; there was something special about working for Stannah.
>
> We started in Andover as just one family playing a part in a Company where family values counted for something. I believe that to this day these values continue to underpin the culture at Stannah.
>
> In 1999, after 25 years with Stannah, I left to run my own business and I have tried to model our culture on the Stannah values. No prizes for guessing why.

IMPROVED STAIRLIFT PRODUCTION METHODS AND DESIGNS

Alan Stannah recalls that while moving stairlift curved rail production from Tiverton Street to Andover solved the space problem, producing the complex curved tubular rails was still a challenge. Norman Anderson visited Jan Hamer in Holland to learn their production methods and set up a clone of this in Andover. Alan comments:

> I was appalled. It looked like a work by Emmett and there was clearly scope for improvement.
>
> John Bovis brought his creativity to bear and devised a system of fixed and movable jigs that simplified and standardised the rail production in a way that still provides the basis for our rail production methods today.
>
> The stairlift carriage design was similarly simplified with a compact control system using our first printed circuit boards. Norman Anderson and the production team responded to these new designs by increasing our output in response to the now increasing sales. It was early days, but this was the beginning of a roll that has continued to the present day.

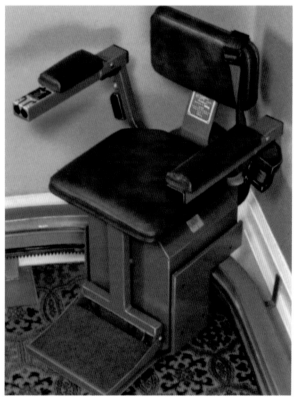

5.9 The first Stannah stairlifts were designed for staircases requiring a curved rail.

GOLDEN *AND* SILVER RAIL

The first stairlifts were suited for a wide range of staircases requiring a curved rail, but it was soon obvious that there was a significant market for a stairlift designed specifically for staircases that would require only a straight rail. With Brian's marketing input, Alan and John Bovis quickly responded with a suitable design which was launched at NAIDEX (National Aids for the Disabled Exhibition) in 1977.

With its extruded aluminium rail allowing efficient production and its compact dimensions arising from its innovative carriage-mounted drive system, Stannah's new straight stairlift was an immediate success.

This new dual product range of straight and curved products helped Stannah Stairlifts Limited to become established as market leaders with what became known as the Golden Rail and Silver Rail stairlifts.

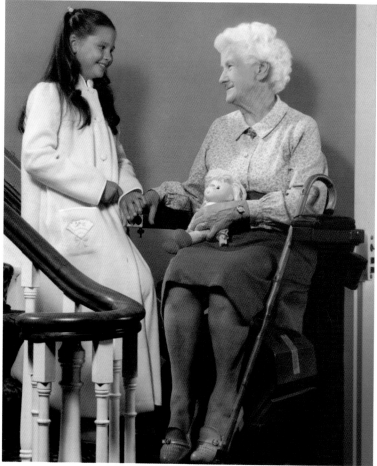

5.10 It soon became obvious that there was a demand for stairlifts for staircases that required only a straight rail.

COMPUTERS AND COMPUTERISED CONTROL

The mid-1970s also saw developments across many aspects of the company including the appointment of Ian Ash, who succeeded Colin Waas and was later appointed to the position of Financial Director. Under his guidance a computerised accounting system was put in place, together with the first steps towards computerising many of the previously paper-based administrative systems. This process proceeded inexorably for many years, as the demands on the centralised computer system multiplied exponentially. New and more powerful computer systems followed one after another, yet incredibly without any increase in the size of the computer room, due to the continuing miniaturisation of the equipment.

Alan Stannah recalls attending early seminars introducing the production planning department to the wonders of materials requirements planning, known as MRP or MRP2.

> A consultant, Gerry David, was appointed to assist us and thankfully he agreed that we would first try to understand the problems to which MRP was the peddled solution.
>
> Just like the 'moans' meetings of old in Tiverton Street, we called in representatives of all of the production departments to listen to their problems and it soon became clear that a better solution would be achieved through new thinking from Japan, including Kanban paperless production scheduling and the revolution in streamlining our production that followed from Just in Time principles.
>
> These systems would take many years to perfect, but as with every journey nothing starts until one has taken that first step.
>
> In parallel with this we were taking the first steps towards computer numerically controlled (CNC) sheet metal punching and bending machines and computer aided design (CAD) in the drawing offices. As with the computer systems, improvements followed year upon year and this trend has continued to the present day.

TRACTION AND HYDRAULIC

As the company grew through the 1970s, the 'new lifts' side of the business was still suffering from the effects of the downturn, and recovery was slow. Indeed, by 1980 sales within the industry for traction passenger lifts had still only recovered to 1,233 from the low point in 1977 of 1,228, compared to the peak of 3,443 in 1973. However, there was one positive trend. Hydraulic passenger lifts had shown almost uninterrupted growth throughout the downturn, from 244 units in 1971 to 733 by 1980, and Alan decided it was time to consider entering this growing market.

With the success of importing Daldoss's Microlifts under their belt, Alan made further trips to Italy and developed relationships with the companies IGV and GMV, both in Milan. At that time, all Stannah's lifts were balanced traction, although, as revealed by the industry statistics, architects were attracted to the low-headroom requirements of hydraulic lifts. The technology did not look too difficult and with help from IGV and, later, GMV, Stannah introduced their own hydraulic lift range. This proved to be a significant milestone in the growth of the lift company. A brochure was produced offering on facing pages two ranges of lifts that were identical in all respects apart from the differing hydraulic and traction drive systems, allowing customers and architects freedom of choice to suit their requirements. It soon became clear that there was a strong trend towards the hydraulic lift, to which the company was well placed to respond. Thus, not for the first time, product development was matched to the market requirement – a continuing theme in the development of the company.

Year	Traction	Hydraulic	Total
1981	1,249	728	1,977
1982	1,448	1,006	2,454
1983	1,129	1,056	2,185
1984	1,087	1,326	2,413
1985	978	1,536	2,514
1986	948	1,952	2,890
1987	1,161	2,284	2,445
1988	1,766	3,079	4,845
1989	1,736	3,320	5,956

(Figures are lifts sold within the industry as a whole.)

GOODS LIFTS AND BED LIFTS

Alan recalls that although the Maxilift and Microlift had developed the sale and production of standard lifts, there was still a reluctance to turn work away. Goods lifts and hospital bed lifts were still produced in small numbers until overtaken by the reality that low levels of production were not commercially viable. The nail in the coffin may have been the adoption of twin telescopic rams on a bed lift, sold to the company by a silver-tongued salesman, leading to endless problems with synchronisation. A system was developed to re-synchronise the hydraulic cylinders by parking the lift on its buffers at night, but this gave Alan too many grey hairs, and Stannah learned its lessons from this that the future lay in large numbers of a more standardised product.

STRUCTURE SUPPORTED HOMELIFTS

In response to the market demands from residential homes, the company developed a wider range of structure-supported Homelifts, the design office bringing this to market within one year. This sold strongly through to the mid-1980s, when technical problems with competitor products gave rise to a change in the Standards requirement for such lifts. Stannah Lifts again responded quickly to these changing market requirements with the introduction of the Piccolo hydraulic passenger lift, allowing sales and production to be maintained.

THE GROWING SERVICE NETWORK

Another of Brian Stannah's key initiatives at this time was to respond to the company's appetite for further acquisitions which had been whetted by their purchases of Southern Lifts and the London Lift Company. Brian was determined to take advantage of any opportunities that arose. This he did, at regular intervals. These were the dates, with Brian's comments:

> 1977 – Bristol Electric Lifts Limited. 'A retirement situation where the partners in a well-run company needed an exit. They preferred us to competing purchasers.'

> 1979 – Castle Group, Bristol. 'Sounds pretentious, but it wasn't. However, a useful input of new business to our Bristol branch.'

> 1982 – Sovereign Lifts Limited, Norwich. 'Owner wanted to go to Australia.'

> 1983 – Dukarran. 'Probably the messiest, but it got our feet on the ground in Birmingham, Mansfield and Manchester.'

> 1984 – R.J. Shaw, Gateshead. 'Another retirement situation. Alan Shaw was nearing retirement, another second generation. A good little company.'

> 1988 – F.M. Bell Limited, Manchester. 'Ian Bell (again second generation) and his company were customers for Microlifts and stairlifts for years, but eventually he wanted out.'

> 2000 – Peter Brown Limited, Glasgow. 'Peter had been our Scottish Distributor, but overstretched himself with mobility aids showrooms in Edinburgh and Glasgow and a depot in Inverness and made unwise property related decisions.'

> 'So, a series of stepping stones which extended our areas of operation with the range of opportunities which arose therefrom.'

However, it was not only by acquisition that Stannah expanded their service network. At that time the Eastbourne Service Branch covered the whole of the south coast – too long a stretch – and this resulted in the opening of a Service Branch in Christchurch, near Bournemouth, to fill the gap between the Eastbourne and Bristol offices.

Pete Perry, the former Managing Director of Stannah Lift Services Ltd (Maintenance and Repair Division), recalls that servicing lifts was a different task in the 1970s and 1980s:

Many of the lifts, whether manufactured by Stannah or other makers, were of an older technology and many of the servicing methods used then would no longer be allowed under today's more stringent rules for the Health and Safety of one's work people. We relied then on experience, which was essential.

The London service business then outgrew its original Tiverton Street building (rebuilt by L.N. Stannah at the end of the Second World War after war damage) and bought a site in Newport Street, Lambeth and commissioned Max Hutchinson, later to become President of the RIBA, to design a three-floor building for their occupation.

5.11 Shortly after the move to Andover, Stannah moved whatever remained at Tiverton Street into new premises in Newport Street, south-east London.

Later that business was split, with moves to Dartford and Crayford and, at the same time, responsibilities for some counties were transferred to a newly opened Branch at Brackley. Nevertheless, the company still owns the building in Newport Street having leased it to a printer who does a great deal of work for the House of Commons just over the river.

On property in general the Stannahs have tried to own as many as possible of the buildings the company uses, and if the local service branch outgrows its premises, still retains them in case of further need while in the meantime renting them to tenants.

DEGREE STUDENTS AND RECRUITMENT

By the late 1970s the company decided to support its long-standing programmes of technician and craft apprenticeships with the recruitment of engineering degree students, to whom support was offered through university sandwich courses which coupled their academic training with valuable industrial experience.

A past joint MD of Stannah Stairlifts Limited was the second recruitment made under this scheme, having joined Stannah in 1980. A number of other students were recruited, but for a variety of reasons these fell by the wayside. However, the value of combining academic training with industrial experience was proved beyond doubt, and since then the company has developed and strengthened these recruitment and training programmes.

5.12 Alan Stannah showing HRH Prince Philip, Duke of Edinburgh, a Stannah stairlift at NAIDEX (National Aids for the Disabled Exhibition) in 1979.

ANOTHER SIGNIFICANT EVENT

With the growth of the Service division in the early 1980s a vacancy arose for an experienced service manager in the Birmingham Branch. Coincidentally, in 1984 Brian Stannah received a letter from Derek Lloyd, who had an immense amount of experience in the lift industry and who had fallen victim to the rationalisation being forced on the industry by the general recession of the early 1980s. Derek was invited for interview and he impressed immediately that he would make a very good fit within the organisation. Never mind service manager, would he consider joining as Director of the Service division? Derek said thank you, yes, he would – so a partnership that was of great benefit to both parties was agreed.

5.13 Derek Lloyd, an immensely experienced lifts manager, joined Stannah in the mid-1980s and organised Stannah's servicing operations throughout the country.

After working for a number of engineering companies in the Midlands in the 1950s and 1960s, in 1972 Lloyd had been appointed a director of Samuel Pegg, a subsidiary of Bentley Engineering, itself a part of the large Charles Clore Sears Group whose main claim to fame was its ownership of Selfridges department store. In 1978 Sears disposed of Bentley Engineering and Lloyd became managing director of Evans Lifts, based in Leicester and by this time part of the Harris and Sheldon Group. Evans was a substantial player in the industry, supplying commercial lifts to Marks and Spencer, lifts for the Thames Barrier and also for Britain's nuclear power stations. In 1981 Harris and Sheldon sold Evans Lifts to the giant Otis and, after a difficult three years, Lloyd found himself rationalised out of the business as Otis merged Evans with other lift manufacturers in its stable.

Otis's loss was Stannah's gain, as Brian Stannah appointed him with the brief to bring cohesion to the many service branches which Stannah was now trying to run throughout the country. As Lloyd put it:

As well as head office and the manufacturing operation at Andover there was the Special Lifts Division in Newport Street in London, Southern Lifts in Eastbourne and servicing branches in Norwich, Manchester, Birmingham, Gateshead and Bristol. They were all doing their own thing and chasing sales without much regard for profit.

I based myself in Birmingham from where I could get to any of the branches and back in a day. Eventually I got them to work as a team and we concentrated on keeping overheads down and maintaining margins. We made a big point to the customers about our availability which was every day of the year including Christmas Day.

We eventually signed up 45,000 service contracts covering not only Stannah's lifts but every other manufacturer's as well. The installations and service contracts that stand out in my memory are:

The lifts we put into the Mansion House in the City and into the DTI building in London and also the ones into the towers on the Severn Bridge. These were all done by the Special Lifts Division in Newport Street.

Then there were the Royal Fleet Auxiliary ships and the servicing of the Cross-Channel ferries from our Norwich office.

The Manchester office started the Railtrack [see later references to Railtrack and Network Rail] contract and it also serviced 12 lifts at Old Trafford. We had no trouble getting the standby engineers to work Saturdays and Sundays for that job!

I was also able to negotiate a contract with Tesco, and, at one time, we were servicing a third of all their stores. Unfortunately we eventually lost that contract to a cheaper quote. (The company always put quality of service foremost, but that comes at a price.)

I also started the second-hand stairlifts division which has been very profitable.

This growth in the 1980s was achieved in the teeth of some very difficult conditions, especially at the

5.14 Stannah lifts were installed in the Mansion House in the City, the DTI building in London, and in the towers on the Severn Bridge.

5.15 The cross-channel ferries were serviced from Stannah's Norwich office.

5.16 At one point Stannah were servicing one third of Tesco's stores.

beginning of the decade, and as Brian Stannah later said: 'Derek Lloyd's contribution was one of the highlights of the time.'

'THE LADY'S NOT FOR TURNING'

Yet another recession hit British industry in 1980. A dramatic change had arrived on the political scene in May 1979 when the electorate, tired of a decade of the collective approach, voted in Margaret Thatcher, a woman who promised a new start. It had been a miserable decade for a once-proud nation. After further sharp slippage down the world's economic league, the country had reached a stage by early 1979 where the prospect was not of decline *relative* to our main competitors, but of *absolute* decline. The country had had enough, and Labour Prime Minister James Callaghan, so recently berated by the *Sun* newspaper for saying 'Crisis, what crisis?' when he arrived back from a conference of world leaders in the Caribbean in the middle of yet another winter of industrial disputes (in fact, Callaghan never said those words, but that was the *Sun*'s headline and everybody believed it), realised that the country wanted a change.

While the unions had been on the rampage in the mid-1970s, the middle classes felt they were in an alien land and agreed with Patrick Hutber, the city editor of the *Sunday Telegraph*, when he wrote in his book, *The Decline and Fall of the Middle Class*:

> That this is a time of crisis for the nation is commonplace, but it is equally a time of crisis for the middle class who are subject to unprecedented pressures, and, at the same time, to unprecedented denigration.

Hutber went on to point out that he felt it was wrong for everyone to be reliant on the state for everything. Finally he pointed out that high taxation discouraged the payment of high salaries. This might be thought of as a social advantage, but in an increasingly international economy it meant that British companies would not attract the best people – and even if they did, it would not give them much incentive to work hard.

While Hutber was attacking socialism and the dreadful damage wrought by inflation, the Tory Party ousted its leader, Edward Heath, who had put in place many of the doctrines of his opponents, the Labour Party – restrictions on wages, prices and dividends. In his place the party elected a woman who, under the tutelage of Sir Keith Joseph, had grasped certain essentials of the remedy required to restore economic sanity to the country.

From February 1975 until she came into power in May 1979, Thatcher and her supporters prepared the ground for a revolution in Britain's economic attitudes. Hugo Young, in his biography, *One of Us*, summed up her position when she assumed power:

She brought to that post no great technical expertise, but a handful of unshakeable principles.

They were not particularly original principles. But they were commitments made with the fire of the zealot who could not imagine she would ever become a bore. Tax cutting was one of them. In four years as Opposition leader, she had hardly made a single economic speech without alluding to the punitive rates of tax. Usually this was in reference to upper rates. 'A country's top rate of tax is a symbol,' she said in February 1978, 'very little revenue is collected from people in this country who pay tax at the highest rates. A top rate of 83 per cent is not much of a revenue raiser. It is a symbol of British socialism – the symbol of envy.' Restoring the morale of management, she said around the same time, was the prime requirement. 'No group is more important, and yet none has been so put through the mangle and flattened between the rollers of progressively penal taxation and discriminatory incomes policy.'

So tax cuts were the first objective. They were the traditional Tory nostrum, to which the leader brought her special proselytising zeal. The second was good housekeeping.

The third fundamental therefore defined itself: the control of public spending. And again a kind of pietistic morality went hand in hand with a supposed economic law.

5.17 Margaret Thatcher, Conservative Prime Minister from 1979 until 1990, did more than any other single person to wake up the British people to the reality of how competitive the world had become. Britain had been declining relatively since the 1950s and was about to decline in absolute terms at the end of the 1970s. By the time she resigned at the end of 1990, the British could hold their heads up again.

The general financial climate from 1980 to 1982 had been the worst since the war, certainly in terms of corporate failures and rising unemployment. The result of tight monetary policies allied to another sharp hike in the price of oil following the overthrow of the Shah in Iran, which in turn brought a sharp rise in the value of the pound, viewed by this time as a petro-currency thanks to Britain's near self-sufficiency in oil from the North Sea, was to create the most difficult trading conditions British companies had experienced since the thirties. ICI, generally viewed as the bell-wether of British manufacturing industry, cut its dividend and Sir Terence

Beckett, the Director-General of the CBI, promised the government a 'bare knuckle fight', saying at the CBI conference: 'We have got to have a lower pound – we've got to have lower interest rates.'

The Prime Minister remained firm and declared on the day unemployment passed the two million mark (Heath had lost his nerve when it passed the one million mark): 'I've been trying to say to people for a very long time; if you pay yourself more for producing less, you'll be in trouble.'

Heavy wage inflation allied to a near-doubling of VAT in the first budget of the new administration (introduced within weeks of their winning power) meant that inflation soared again to an average 13.3 per cent in 1979, 18.1 per cent in 1980 and 11.9 per cent in 1981. Thereafter it fell to under 5 per cent in time for the general election of 1983, aided by the overvalued pound and moderate wage settlements induced by an unemployment level not seen since the thirties.

At the same time, a very tough attitude towards unions and strikes epitomised by the government's approach to a national strike in the steel industry – a strike they were determined to win whatever the cost – meant that the government's and Thatcher's popularity fell to new depths by the end of 1981. But Thatcher pressed on regardless, and although she had invited people from the whole spectrum of the party into her cabinet, she took little notice of what many of them said. Indeed she made it quite clear that:

> If you're going to do the things you want to do – and I'm only in politics to do things – you've got to have a togetherness and a unity in your cabinet. There are two ways of making a cabinet. One way is to have in it people who represent all the different viewpoints within the party, within the broad philosophy. The other way is to have in it only people who want to go in the direction in which every instinct tells me we have to go. Clearly, steadily, firmly, with resolution. We've got to go in an agreed and clear direction.

She was not going to 'waste time having any internal arguments'.

Not that Thatcher and her Conservative government worked instant miracles. Indeed, the country was immediately plunged into another inflationary crisis as more trouble in the Middle East, including the deposing of the Shah of Iran, led to another sharp rise in the price of oil. This was exacerbated by Thatcher agreeing to implement in full the awards recommended by the Clegg Commission, set up in the so-called 'winter of discontent' to grant a whole new raft of inflationary wage settlements. The belief of the new administration in increasing indirect taxing and reducing direct taxation did not help in the short term either, as Chancellor of the Exchequer Sir Geoffrey Howe virtually doubled the rate of VAT from 8 to 15 per cent in his budget introduced in June 1979.

However, throughout this turmoil Stannah continued its steady development, extending territory, improving and introducing new products, and strengthening its services portfolio and its asset base.

PUBLICITY

Stannah first invested in public and press relations in 1976 and became involved briefly with an agency that brought them such characters as Professor Heinz Wolff and Dr Christiaan Barnard, the world-famous heart-transplant surgeon, to endorse their products.

In the early 1980s a publicity consultancy, Abucon, run by Liza Jones, wrote to Brian Stannah offering their services and were appointed. In January 1986 Liza wrote a lengthy press release, and it gives a fascinating snapshot of Stannah Lifts at that time – how it saw itself and how it wanted to project itself.

In the opening paragraph it claimed the origins of the company to have been in the 1830s. It went on to give a brief history of the company through the second half of the 19th century and on into the 20th, up to the 1980s when Stannah's service became national:

> In early 1984, the local branches in Birmingham, Manchester and Nottingham were expanded when the Dukarran Lift company became part of the Stannah Group. This brought an improved lift service to customers in the Midlands and the North of England and was a move particularly welcomed by elderly and disabled people who were then able to obtain more immediate help from the team of trained Stannah engineers.
>
> R.J. Shaw and Company, a family run Newcastle-upon-Tyne lift business employing half a dozen people, joined the Stannah fold in July 1985, and later a production unit was established to manufacture rails for Stannah's Golden Rail stairlift in the Dunston premises, resulting in a number of additional staff being recruited.

5.18 Brian and Alan Stannah in the Andover factory in the 1980s.
By this time, stairlifts were providing strong growth for the company.

By this time, stairlifts were providing strong growth for the company, and Abucon made sure that their best features, especially safety, were fully understood:

The first stairlift produced by Stannah for people with mobility problems was the GOLDEN RAIL Stairlift in 1975. This is a motorised chair which glides along a slim curved rail at the side of the staircase.

It can be installed quickly and efficiently, even on a steep staircase. The Golden Rail is neat and unobtrusive, fixed to the floor and folding away when not in use.

The Golden Rail has an unrivalled range of safety features including a special pad under the footrest which responds to obstructions arising from any of four different directions. Stannah believe this unique feature will ensure Golden Rail provides significantly greater protection than any other stairlift.

In the past, the Stannah Golden Rail has been installed in a number of usual and not so usual sites. By far the most frequent request is for a Golden Rail in the home. But some of the more interesting applications can be found in children's playbuses, museums and colleges.

The Stannah ACCESS WHEELCHAIR STAIRLIFT, with its sturdy platform, carries the wheelchair-bound passenger safely up and down a flight of stairs without assistance.

The latest model is compact enough for many domestic locations. It requires no structural alterations and thus often solves the stairclimbing problem for wheelchair passengers in the most economical way. The motor is incorporated in the unit and the platform folds up when not in use, leaving the stairs clear and safe for other users.

Options include a side ramp and a pendant control, allowing a severely handicapped passenger's attendant to walk beside the lift and control its travel.

Those confined to a wheelchair but with use of their arms, can easily wheel themselves on to the 'Access' platform, use the simple joy-stick controls, and take a brief ride to the top or bottom of the staircase.

Administrators of public buildings were quick off the mark to realise the potential of 'Access'. One of the first sites was the Bloomsbury Theatre, part of the University College, London. Two 'Access' Stairlifts now throw open the theatre's many facilities to wheelchair users.

However, the release was not all about stairlifts:

For those who prefer conventional vertical travel there is the Stannah 'HOMELIFT' range. Carrying two to four people, or a wheelchair-bound passenger plus attendant, Homelifts have all the benefits of larger commercial lifts, but are conveniently 'home sized'.

The Homelift needs no load-bearing wall or support shaft, and only occupies the space of a cupboard. Options include power assisted landing doors, low level push buttons and an internal car seat.

Safety and security, as well as customer satisfaction, were always priorities for the Stannahs, as is shown by the following:

> Stannah ensure that customers receive expert advice BEFORE making their final choice of lift. And with this in mind, they employ a fully qualified Occupational Therapist and a State Registered Nurse who can help customers with any queries they may have.
>
> All sales staff strictly adhere to the company policy of only selling a stairlift or other type of domestic lift if it is genuinely suitable for that particular site or disability.

Of course, the Stannahs were fully aware of all the psychological barriers to people admitting that their life would be improved by the installation of a stairlift.

> Some of the most commonly heard sentiments come from elderly people, suffering from arthritis, heart trouble or who may be recovering from a stroke. Once the lift is installed, they can move around their homes unaided and still have space to accommodate their grandchildren when they come to stay. So much better than the upheaval and expense of a move to smaller, single storey premises.
>
> One such example is Mrs Meek of Gloucestershire. Mrs Meek has a heart complaint which for many years meant she was confined to the ground floor of the cottage in which she was born. Her staircase was unusually steep, but now she has a Silver Rail stairlift installed.

5.19 Brian and Alan in front of a stairlift test-rig.

'After spending 20 years downstairs living in one room the stairlift has opened up the whole of my house to me,' said Mrs Meek. 'Now I have my real bedroom back. And an added bonus, I have found things upstairs that I had completely forgotten about!'

Parents with disabled children have also benefited from Stannah stairlifts. Carrying a growing child up a flight of stairs several times a day can place a heavy burden on families, especially when there are other children also demanding attention.

Because of their provision of items that helped the handicapped and the disabled, the Stannahs were only too well aware of the problems faced every day by such people, and, as Abucon pointed out, were active in helping in every way they could:

High unemployment has hit the disabled workforce even harder than the rest of the community. At the end of 1984, however, the British Government published its 'Code of Good Practice on the Employment of Disabled People'. The wealth of information contained in this code provides employers with helpful advice on employing disabled people.

The Royal Association for Disability and Rehabilitation (RADAR) has kept the ball rolling since 1984 with their 'Employability' campaign to win more jobs for the disabled.

Stannah Lifts, along with an ever-increasing number of caring companies, have long since been aware of the fact that employees do a job well because of their abilities, NOT their disabilities.

Stannah have a positive policy towards employing disabled people, encouraging applications from disabled people and retaining on their staff those employees who may become disabled during their working life.

In addition, Stannah give simple assembly work to the Andover Adult Training Centre, where mentally handicapped people, some with physical problems as well, continue their education. Here each individual works to his or her own programme, which is carefully tailored to their capabilities and potential. It is a great boost to their morale when they assemble components which are later used in Stannah's factory assembly line, as they feel they are really doing a worthwhile job of work. Just another example of how Stannah take into account the needs of all members of a community.

Stannah provided not only sponsorship for activities that helped the disabled but also practical help:

In the early 1980s Stannah designed and installed special lifts in the *Soren Larsen*, a vessel commissioned by the Jubilee Sailing Trust and adapted so that it could be manned by a crew, half of which were disabled.

On a purely commercial basis, Stannah were selected by the Trust to supply lifts so that the disabled crew members could move safely and independently between the decks.

Stannah were very impressed with the efforts being made by the Trust. So, when the vessel returned to dry dock after the first season at sea, they undertook a number of modifications and refurbishment to the lifts free of charge as their contribution to the venture. They have continued their maintenance and development pledge and have also underlined their confidence in the project by contributing £1,500 [in today's money about £6,000] to the Charity's funds.

The Trust was so pleased with Stannah's work on the *Soren Larsen* that they returned to this manufacturer when it came to nominating a company to design and develop lifts for their new vessel, the *Lord Nelson*, which was launched in October 1985.

The Riding for the Disabled Association (RDA) is another organisation to which Stannah have given support. This charity has been striving to bring the benefits and pure fun of riding to as many disabled people as possible since 1969.

RDA's work increases the confidence and often results in medical improvement in the individual disabled riders. There are now some 600 groups, each complete with their own organiser, instructor and willing band of voluntary workers bringing happiness to more than 20,000 disabled riders nationwide.

But as with any charity, funds are a problem. On a day-to-day basis, RDA groups have to cope with riding school fees, vet and feed bills. Stannah were only too pleased to help, and for the last six years have sponsored the sales of RDA Christmas cards.

THE PERSONALITY AND FLAVOUR OF THE INDUSTRY

In 1982, William (Bill) Sturgeon, the editor of the American magazine catering for the US lift industry, *Elevator World*, visited the UK and, with the help of the staff of the National Association of Lift Makers (NALM), spent nearly six weeks visiting all the UK's leading lift manufacturers.

On his visit to Stannah in Andover, Sturgeon, *inter alia*, wrote this:

Day 18 – Andover
Stannah Lifts

The morning has always been the most important part of my day; rising early and reading the newspapers thoroughly to digest the state of the outer world before settling down to one's own activities. Nowhere can this be better done than in London where there must be the world's widest choice of newspapers – perhaps a dozen in all. The pleasure of catching up on events is compounded by indulging in the snug enjoyment of an 'English train breakfast': linen table cloth, a setting of the country's famed china, warm plates, rolls, honey, your own jar of Frank Cooper's 'Oxford' coarse-cut marmalade and a choice of eggs, bacon, sausage, crunchy fried bread, grilled tomatoes and mushrooms and plenty of hot coffee – made according to British Rail's own secret recipe. Life is complete; leisurely dividing the hour and a half to Andover between reading the papers, gorging and drinking in the country-side, unbelievably green even without a drop of rain in the previous three weeks. The fruit trees are in full bloom, the train speeds along, and one reflects upon the golden days of travelling on the New York Central's 'Twentieth Century Limited' and 'Commodore Vanderbilt' between Manhattan and Buffalo or Chicago – those luxurious saloons of yesteryear with solicitous personnel one longs for increasingly, now that airline passengers are processed like Coca-Cola. Thankfully, the UK has preserved good rail service, the English breakfast and a wide choice of newspapers. All combine to make the morning trip memorable … Upon arriving at the plant I am greeted by Brian Stannah, co-director of the firm with brother, Alan.

Sturgeon was certainly impressed by all the efforts of Liza Jones at Abucon, writing in the report of his round-the-lift-industry journey to celebrate the 50th anniversary of NALM:

I ferreted out one 'secret weapon' [Alan was being careful of telling him about new developments at Stannah], that old American development, 'public relations'. We had been joined by Liza Jones, Stannah's Public Relations Consultant, up from London for the day, and as she and her employer detailed the programs formulated over the years, the information began to pour out. They were so enthused about their newsletters, direct mailing systems, newspaper, mailing lists and advertising in newspapers, magazines and on radio and TV, there was no way it would be suppressed. The company has a communications program which would be envied in any country (and on Madison Avenue). Of course, lift applications for the handicapped or elderly lend themselves particularly, to exposure. There are photographs of such units in castles and rest homes, being used by dignitaries (including a trial spin by HRH Prince Charles, Patron of the International Year for Disabled People), comments by Professor Christiaan Barnard, the famous [heart] surgeon, concerning the use of stairlifts etc.

Much of this is consolidated in the *Stannah News* which is mailed to organisations for elderly people, Social Service Departments, doctors and others who might have an interest in a lift. To ensure the equipment is properly placed and utilised, Stannah has recruited a staff of field representatives. A photo indicates an equal representation of men and women. Several have had experience as occupational therapists or working with Social Services.

Liza Jones said of the company's logo:

Part of our campaign was a new logo – a bird on the wing; a far cry from the usual company formats based on directional arrows or mechanical designs. It depicts

'Freedom'. We want people to see our ideas and equipment as a means of achieving mobility.

THE END OF AN ERA

As the 1970s drew to a close, so did Pop's life, and he died peacefully on 9 April 1979 aged 77 (he was born 18 December 1901). He would have been very content with the business that he had resurrected at the end of the Second World War, now flourishing and evidently set for a growing future. Today he is remembered with fondness by those who knew him, and at formal occasions the first toast is 'To Pop'. However, it is said that behind every good man is a good woman, and the love and support given by Jean as wife and mother should not be forgotten. Rather like the unseen part of an iceberg, so her contribution to the partnership went largely unmarked. However, as Brian and Alan now acknowledge, Pop's post-war achievements were probably only possible with the back-up she gave to the family. Jean followed Pop, dying, again peacefully, at home at Old Bosham on 23 December 1989. After Pop's death, Alan, who lived nearby, was able to keep an eye on 'Mother', for which Brian has always been grateful.

We should not finish remembering Pop Stannah without recalling his younger brother, Colin, born on 11 December 1911, ten years after Pop.

5.20 Colin Stannah on his motorcycle in the 1920s.

5.21 Colin with his father, A.J. Stannah.

During his early years, much of his time was spent with the hired help and he often ate meals with them in the kitchen. He was educated (as was Pop) at the City of London School and, leaving early, applied for an apprenticeship with the Otis Elevator Company. On completion of this apprenticeship he and a friend, Alex McWhirter, applied for positions being offered to start up Otis offices in Kenya and South Africa. They tossed for who went where and Colin got Kenya, moving there in 1934 when he was 23. He proceeded to establish Waygood Otis in Kenya.

During the Second World War he served in the forces in Mombasa, Madagascar and Burma, and by the end of the war he had attained the rank of Major.

After the war, the Kenya operation of Waygood Otis was taken over by the British trading company, Dalgety, and Colin was appointed to their engineering division. Subsequently, he became Head of this division and, as Dalgety dropped the Otis business, concentrated on the sale and servicing of McKinnon's coffee

171

*5.22 Colin and his wife, Nella. They married in 1938 and had been together
for 67 years when Colin died, at the age of 93, in October 2005.*

machinery and Marshall's tea machinery. His job entailed a great deal of travelling throughout East Africa, the Belgian Congo, Rwanda and Burundi. He was particularly successful in the French colonies, where his ability to speak French (he had spent many holidays with a French aunt) stood him in good stead with the French-speaking farmers and merchants.

In the early 1970s, Dalgety was acquired by Smith McKenzie & Co. and this prompted Colin to move back to Otis, where he joined the Board of Otis East Africa Ltd. By the time he left Kenya in 1983 he had been both Managing Director and Chairman of Otis East Africa. While in Kenya, Colin had also founded Showcase International in Nairobi, marketing a range of Australian products including windmills. His son, Dudley, worked at Amazon Motors in Nairobi and Colin became involved in that business as well. Finally, he had also joined the Police Reserve during the Mau Mau emergency. Dudley until recently was General Manager East Africa of Subaru Kenya in Nairobi.

On the sporting front Colin played tennis, squash and soccer. He was president of the Kenya Squash Rackets Association for six years and also President of the Kenya Lawn Tennis Association in 1969–70. He was very proud of the fact that in 1957, at the age of 45, he won the Kenya Open Squash Championship, defeating a player twenty years younger in the final.

In 1960, Colin was inducted into the Rotary Club of Nairobi and he became a passionate Rotarian. He was the prime mover in setting up and running the

5.23 Colin with his son, Dudley.

5.24 In 1968, Dudley Stannah married
Mary Borwick.

Jacaranda School for the mentally handicapped. He later served as President of the Nairobi Rotary Club and, when he moved to South Africa, transferred to the Aurora Rotary Club in Benoni. There he was the driving force behind the establishment of a library and a clinic in the black township of Daveytown near Benoni. He was also a prime mover in the Iceberg Project which sought to ensure that all children in the area were inoculated against tuberculosis. Dudley has followed in his footsteps.

The Benoni *City Times* published an obituary on 28 October 2005. Among other things, it said:

Prominent Benoni businessman and Rotarian, Colin Stannah, died in his sleep on October 12, at the age of 93.

Colin enjoyed travelling and his work with Dalgety's took him to all parts of East and Central Africa.

During World War Two, he served with the British forces in Madagascar, Burma and Kenya, and was always proud of the fact that he danced with Vera Lynn, the 'Forces' Sweetheart'.

In 1967/70 he was made president of the Nairobi Rotary Club, co-incidentally the same year that his wife, Nella, was president of Inner Wheel, an achievement that has never been repeated since.

Colin and Nella moved to South Africa in 1984, where he continued to play an active role as a member of the Benoni Rotary Club.

He would spend weeks working on community projects in Daveytown, Hammanskraal and Rynpark.

Colin's contribution was recognised when he was awarded Rotary's Paul Harris Fellowship on two occasions.

He is survived by Nella, to whom he was married 67 years, son Dudley, daughter-in-law Mary and family in Kenya, and daughter Jackie, son-in-law Aris Kypris and family in Benoni. [At the time of his death he had six grandchildren and five great-grandchildren.]

And this was the tribute paid to him by Brian Stannah in the 2005 edition of *Elevation*:

My uncle, Colin Stannah, died in his sleep on 12 October 2005 at his home near Johannesburg aged 94. He was the younger brother of 'Pop' (Leslie N. Stannah), father to Alan and myself.

Born in 1911, ten years after Pop, Colin was one of those special people who ventured overseas to seek their fortune in one of our former colonies.

A top tennis player, he relinquished the opportunity to play at Wimbledon, instead becoming an entrepreneur in Kenya – at that time a land of opportunity. Game hunter, trader, farmer and finally, believe it or not, he became Managing Director and then Chairman of Otis East Africa.

The wheel had turned full circle and he returned to the family business roots – albeit with another company. I spent happy times with him at his home in Nairobi together with his family, my Aunt Nella and their offspring – our cousins Dudley and Jackie.

When our Queen and Prince Philip spent their honeymoon at Treetops, Colin was amongst those who welcomed them to Kenya at the Muthaiga Club in Nairobi. In 1983, Colin and Nella moved to South Africa to spend their golden years near to their daughter Jackie, and her husband Aris. In fact, they lived next door to each other in the countryside outside Johannesburg and not too far from the racetrack which hosted the South African Grand Prix.

Colin was a larger than life character of immense presence, who walked tall and left a long shadow. If someone were to write his biography it would, I am sure, be a best seller. Whilst not involved in the family business, he had a close interest in Pop's early endeavours in the Post-War years and later set me an example which I am proud to have tried to follow.

Colin leaves his wife Nella (of 67 years' marriage), son Dudley and his wife Mary, daughter Jackie and her husband Aris, together with their six grandchildren.

I feel an era has passed, a generation ended and the mantle of patriarch has folded around my shoulders. I am sure Alan will join me in aspiring to live up to the examples of Pop and Colin.

I think I, at least, will have to grow a long white beard …!

CHAPTER SIX

1985–1989

STEADY GROWTH

EXPORT-LED GROWTH AND THE FIRST OVERSEAS DISTRIBUTORS MEETINGS
LIFT ELECTRONIC CONTROLS AND MICROPROCESSORS
NOTHING VENTURED NOTHING GAINED
THE QUEEN'S AWARD FOR EXPORT ACHIEVEMENT
THE PERFORMANCE PLAN – SHARING IN GROWTH

EXPORT-LED GROWTH AND THE FIRST OVERSEAS DISTRIBUTORS MEETINGS

In the 1970s the company realised that with its new stairlifts products it had happened on a growth market and poured more and more resources into it. Brian appointed Gilbert Advertising, an agency in the Strand in London, and, after handling the selling himself, took on a neighbour and bridge friend, Mike Robinson. Robinson was Sales Manager at Marshall Conveyors and Brian was struck by his commitment and long evenings spent planning the next day's sales activity. At the same time, Brian Stannah felt there must be export potential, and he travelled the world in the late 1970s and early 1980s setting up distributorships. His technique for meeting potential distributors was simple but effective. He would book himself into the best hotel in town, advertise his presence in the most important business newspaper and invite potential distributors to come and talk to him and see what he was offering.

This is how Brian Stannah remembers it:

I suppose the motivation to try for sales overseas came from our Microlifts experience in two ways. Our Italian principal, Daldoss, was an exporter and he had what I would have described as a 'cardboard box product'. For the first time in 1978 with our Silver Rail stairlift, so did we. Just two options – left and right hand and cut the rail to length yourself. The obvious starting point was the list of Microlift Distributors in other European countries. Easy targets, as we had a common interest and that quickly paid off – Holland being particularly successful through a partnership with Starlift (the largest lift manufacturer in Holland).

Perhaps their greatest success has been in Germany (until the 1990s, West Germany). Harald Seick, the Managing Director of Lifta, Stannah's German distributor, recalled how Brian Stannah wrote to his father Wolfgang in 1978:

> Brian wrote to a number of potential distributors in Germany. I believe my father was the only one who responded. He felt an empathy towards stairlifts because his mother is handicapped. He agreed to take over the distribution but only in the area of Cologne. Initially things moved slowly because, although stairlifts were not strictly regulated elsewhere, they certainly were in Germany.

Alan Stannah, who was involved in the development of the British Standard for Stairlifts from the outset, comments that at that time the TUV (Technischer Überwachungsverein, i.e. Technical Inspection Association) in Germany did indeed set the most rigorous technical requirements.

As the years have passed the differing national requirements have become more aligned, although it was not until 2009 that a harmonised European Standard for Stairlifts was finally published. Representatives from the Stannah companies have been involved in the ongoing development of these standards, as is described in later chapters.

This is how Brian Stannah remembers the beginnings of the German distributorship:

> Germany was another kettle of fish, as there was no Microlifts Distributor there. Germany was traditionally divided into its Lander, each with its regional city – Stuttgart, Munich, Frankfurt and Hanover being examples – and we felt we'd need a Distributor in each region.
>
> So I set off in my Mercedes Benz (a good choice for the prospective market) with a Silver Rail stairlift in the boot having made appointments with companies in a number of regions. Arriving at Cologne I met Hopmann GmbH, owned and run by Herr Wolfgang Seick, aided by two of his sons, Thomas and Stefan.
>
> A rapport instantly developed, but it wasn't easy as Germany had stringent technical rules and standards enforced by the TUV and compliance would need design changes and submissions for approvals to be made. These took two years, but by the beginning of the 1980s, the product was ready for the market. Soon after a third

6.1 *The Seick family. L to R: Thomas, Harald, Wolfgang and Stefan.*

6.2 *Some years later, Thomas and Harald with Axel Jaschek and Hartmut Bulling.*

Seick son came on the scene. I'd met Harald before having skied with the family in Switzerland, but now he decided to join the family firm and Seick Senior offered him the challenge of taking the stairlift to market, initially just in the Cologne region. However, Harald proved to be a born entrepreneur, formed a new company, Lifta, and quickly achieved National coverage. 2018 will mark 40 years of the partnership between the two family businesses.

Harald himself was still at university at this time, but he gradually became involved. He recalls:

I went on a trip to Australia and I was lying on the beach when I thought, 'I should be selling stairlifts.'

So, in 1982 we started in earnest. I placed some small ads. We received 200 replies and followed up all of them. About ten per cent were really interested and

6.3 The marketing of Lifta, Stannah's German distributor, was of the highest order.

we converted about half of those into orders. In the end in 1982 we received about 50 orders. In that year the distributors Brian had appointed in Hamburg and Bavaria sold nothing so I took over the whole country and, at the same time set up a special company for selling stairlifts, Lifta. We never looked back. Here are the German sales numbers showing the growth in the first few years:

1981 – 5
1982 – 52
1983 – 250 – and in this year we started our own service division
1984 – 410
1985 – 520
1986 – 630

Brian continues:

Concurrently other new markets were entered whilst maintaining regular contact with existing Distributors. This was no mean task that was only relieved after 1989 when newly appointed Stairlifts Managing Director, David Walton, started to share the load. Pride is a dreadful sin, but I enjoy telling our monthly induction groups of new employees how much pleasure I gain from knowing that some of the containers bringing televisions, motor bikes and computers from Japan return laden with our stairlifts.

Our relationship with Chuo (our Japanese partner) started in 1982. I have always gained satisfaction from the company's initial entry into the Japanese market in 1982 and more particularly from the long term relationship which has evolved thereafter. At first the connection with Chuo was via an intermediary in Tokyo, a trading agent,

6.4 During the 1980s, Brian Stannah travelled the world to set up other distributorships. The strain was relieved when David Walton (left) was appointed Stairlifts Managing Director.

familiar with import procedures, and we had no direct contact with Chuo and thus no dialogue with them about the many commercial and technical topics which effective co-operation would later depend upon. Within a year or so it became clear that the agency was one link too many in the chain and that Stannah and Chuo would benefit from a direct relationship for future progress to be made. A diplomatic process was needed. An impartial marketing consultancy was employed and fortuitously recommended the desired outcome, which led to grateful thanks to the trading agency who departed graciously and the close relationship with Shigenobu Fukuda and his company, Chuo, of which he was the President, started to form. At that time Chuo were Tokyo based lift manufacturers with a number of branch offices in other cities and stairlifts were new to them. However, as will be seen later, their staff responded to the challenges posed by new technology and markets.

Thereafter I made regular visits every three to six months, instigating the required responses being of key importance.

6.5, 6.6 Stannah's relationship with Chuo Elevators in Japan began in 1982.

Doing business with them has been a rewarding and satisfying experience and, strangely perhaps, I found much in common with Shigenobu Fukuda, who showed honourable principles much similar to Herr Wolfgang Seick, both having an extremely strong work ethic into their later years. Shige continued to attend his office daily into his mid 70s despite recovering from a stroke, but sadly died in August 2016. Now his son Kenji and Patrick are enjoying taking the relationship forward on behalf of the next generation. I well recall the first inwards visit made on behalf of Chuo by their Chief Engineer, Mr Yamamoto. He was the bearer of a gift from Shige, a beautiful Japanese lady in kimono in a glass case some 300mm high. He travelled in Economy class and was so concerned about the safety of the gift that it remained on his knees for the duration of the eleven hour flight from Tokyo.

We had a number of stabs at the North American market. One of the first was through R.J. Mobility, a dealer in Chicago, Bob Jackson, himself in a wheelchair. Cash-flow problems finished him. However, during a visit he took me to the look-out floor at the top of the Sears Tower. Back down on the ground we ran into an elevator maintenance crew and Bob Jackson from his wheelchair called out 'Hey guys, I've a Limey lift engineer with me'. Thanks Bob. I was given a conducted tour of the machine rooms of the elevators of what was (between 1973 and 2004) the World's tallest building, 1,450 ft high and 110 storeys. I then formed an association with American Stair-Glide in Kansas City. They made their own straight rail stairlifts, but our Silver Rail was added to their range as a premium product and our Golden Rail gave them a curved capability for the first time. However, foolishly we licenced our technology to them and soon after the relationship foundered.

The 1980s was a very exciting decade for the company. Alan Stannah remembers it like this:

Our company growth rate at this time was meteoric with growing market share, new products and new markets. The modern term for the latter is adjacencies, but in those days I used to refer to it as 'opening doors into empty rooms' and the empty rooms abounded and compounded one upon another. Brian was busy travelling the World opening Distributorships throughout Europe, the Far East and from Iceland to Australia – each one bringing its new flow of orders.

At the same time we were developing our products, as we have already seen through our Maxilift passenger lifts (both traction and hydraulic), including a structure supported version which has since sold strongly. Also a new range of structure supported Homelifts, Golden Rail (curved stairlifts) and Silver Rail (straight stairlifts) and later the compact Piccolo hydraulic passenger lifts – each new product opening doors to new sales opportunities.

As we gained experience of the stairlift market, it was apparent that there would be further opportunities if we could extend the scope of application of the stairlift by introducing swivelling chairs, both manual and powered.

We also introduced ranges of hinged rails, again both manual and powered, that removed the obstruction at the bottom of the staircase caused by the projecting rail and thus widening the sales potential of our stairlifts. Through each of these we opened doors into new rooms and kept our growth dynamic.

Initially it was enough to make a stairlift with a hammer paint finish, at first just silver, then golden brown for Golden Rail and silver for Silver Rail. However, in the home environment we needed to do better than this, so we appointed our first design consultants, Russell Manoy, to improve our designs. Tastes were different then, resulting in a brown and orange colour scheme – but then at home I did have brown carpets and in one room an orange ceiling, so maybe the designer was in step with current trends.

Having supplied lifts to Terence Conran's [now Sir Terence Conran] 'Habitat' stores, the Conran Design Group were probably the best known design house at the time, and so when we decided to appoint a top-class design studio to move our designs further forward the Conran Design Group was a natural choice and with them we developed a new range of chairs for our stairlifts and ran two projects with them to improve our lift car designs. Again, both of these improved our market potential and kept our growth buoyant. The success of the Conran project can be seen through the DNA of their chair design still being evident in the Stannah Stairlifts Sarum chair which we sold through to its retirement in 2016, some 30 years later.

6.7 During the 1980s, Stannah appointed the design consultants, Russell Manoy, to improve their designs.

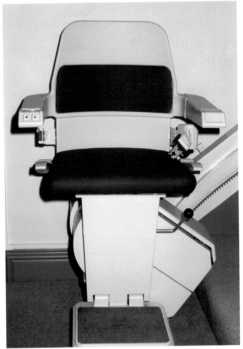

6.8 (right) Having supplied lifts to Terence Conran's Habitat stores, Stannah also used the Conran Design Group to move their designs further forward.

On the production front, Alan Stannah pressed ahead with new developments in order to keep pace with the growth in sales. He said later:

> From there, it was a story of rapid and continued growth. New sections of factory were added in Andover and the company set up a factory in Swansea, where it made Silver Rail carriages and other components and also in Dunston, followed by Blaydon near Newcastle upon Tyne. There an expanding Golden Rail production was set up using the skills of the local workforce for whom fabrication on stairlift rails was relatively light weight after their work in the shipyards.
>
> We adapted to the wonders of numerical control and high-speed punching machines. These changes have continued to the present day with new and even more productive sheet metal working machines and robot welders, keeping our factories at the forefront of modern manufacturing technology. For both Lifts and Stairlifts the introduction of electronic control systems has been a severe challenge, but this is now paying dividends in improved reliability and reduced cost.

The growth is illustrated in the sales and profit numbers.

In 1976, sales had been just over £800,000, gross profit £101,000, and profit before tax £41,000. Even by 1980, sales had grown to £4.2 million, more than five times the 1976 number. And in the 1980s both sales and profits took off, so that in 1989 turnover was £37 million. It was a long way from the turnover of £143,000 of 1969, twenty years earlier, and a very long way from the difficulties of the early 1960s.

Their first Overseas Distributors Meeting (ODM) took place at a hotel on Poole quay. This was so successful that a larger one was organised at Tylney Hall, near Basingstoke, in 1987. Alan Stannah recalls:

6.9 After a first Overseas Distributors Meeting in a hotel on the quayside in Poole, Stannah organised a second one at the prestigious Tylney Hall in 1987, where, among other products, they introduced the Conran-designed stairlifts.

At Tylney Hall we introduced the new Conran chairs, swivel seats, hinged rails, a new Piccolo passenger lift and the Triad mini-bathroom. We also showed new ideas for the future of the curved rail stairlift, Model 220, which later went to full production as 229, and a flat rail design that never made it as we later had better ideas. There was also the Access wheelchair stairlift.

LIFT ELECTRONIC CONTROLS AND MICROPROCESSORS

Alan continues:

At Tylney Hall we also proudly displayed our new lift microprocessor controller which had been introduced on our lifts a year earlier. Previously, Stannah Lifts had been controlled by conventional relay logic. Electronic controls had been in limited use in the lift industry since the 1970s, Alan having experienced the first faltering trials with Mullard Norbit electronic switches during his apprenticeship. However, by the 1980s, the microprocessor became more widely available and understood and microprocessor based lift control systems became the norm. Their introduction was not without difficulty, as fault finding was not as intuitive or obvious as on the older relay based systems and it was a long, hard and frustrating road before reliability was assured. At Tylney Hall all that was in the future and the new microprocessor lift controls were launched in a glow of optimism that was nice while it lasted.

6.10 Stannah embarked on other ventures in the 1980s, including Wessex Trailers. It was not a successful diversification.

NOTHING VENTURED NOTHING GAINED

Alan remembers some other projects of the time:

Along the road other ventures have been tested. Each might have become its own success story and was worth the enthusiasm and effort given. They are worth a brief mention as failure can be as important as success if lessons are learned.

Farm trailers

Looking back, why on earth did we become involved with a couple of farmers down in the West Country who had designed an improved back door system for silage trailers and were making and selling them to local farmers. Maybe we had excess fabrication capacity at the time – the early 1980s. Paul Clifton (mentioned elsewhere herein) drew up the designs, taking the information direct from a trailer, and one of the farmers (the other wanted to retire or at least get out of manufacturing) was retained to sell the product by direct cold calling. It proved to be a fiasco. Sales were not produced in sufficient numbers and the product, in service, had design flaws. End of story.

Triad

We were approached in the early 1980s with the offer of a design for a personal hygiene system for people with impaired mobility comprising shower, WC and washbasin in one unit with ease of access and movement. It was thought it would appeal to many stairlift users and thus would enjoy marketing synergy. Construction was in glass reinforced plastic and the moulds had already been produced.

We took the production, created promotional material, an advertising campaign supported by launch, press and exhibition activity. It bombed and we never understood why. We received sales leads aplenty at lower cost than for stairlifts. The conversion to order was unacceptably low and it was decided the product was unviable. However, the interesting fact was that satisfaction level among those that did buy the product was very high. Maybe the sales advisers at the time needed better training support. We'll never know.

6.11 Another new product, sold under the Stannah name, was the Triad, a personal hygiene system for people with impaired mobility, comprising a shower, WC and washbasin in one unit. Again, sales did not reach an economically viable level.

Flightmaster

Flightmaster was a Silver Rail stairlift derivation designed to transport materials rather than a passenger and was intended as another string to the bow of the Microlift sales team. Demand was not great and there were concerns with safety for stairlift users when a load became displaced and fell and it was withdrawn in the late 1980s.

Air tube conveyors

Somehow our Lifts business acquired the business of a failing company believing that synergy with the Microlift combined with our sales and marketing skills could make this a profitable venture. Duncan LeFeuvre could never be accused of being less than one hundred per cent committed in anything he did, but this failed to gain sufficient momentum and in the late 1980s was allowed to die a death.

Lifting chairs and scooters

In our dealings with distributors for stairlifts in North America we came across armchairs with powered lifting seats and whilst running our newly acquired distributor in Holland, Jon Stannah came across battery powered mobility scooters which were of Japanese origin. Unlike Triad, no manufacture was involved. However, the same degree of promotion and sales was needed and the appropriate effort and enthusiasm was given, but neither were successful and were consequently dropped.

THE QUEEN'S AWARD FOR EXPORT ACHIEVEMENT

A milestone event that coincided with the Tylney Hall meeting was when we were presented with our first Queen's Award for Export Achievement during a presentation ceremony at our Watt Close head office in Andover. The presentation was made by The Deputy Lord Lieutenant of the County of Hampshire, Rear Admiral Sir Morgan Morgan-Giles, in a stirring presentation which was attended by as many of our work people as possible.

The award scheme was instituted by Royal Warrant in 1966 following the recommendations of a committee chaired by HRH the Duke of Edinburgh. Originally introduced as the Queen's Award to Industry, it was replaced in 1976 by two separate awards – the Queen's Award for Export Achievement and the Queen's Award for Technological Achievement.

Her Majesty the Queen makes the awards on the advice of the Prime Minister, who is assisted by an Advisory Committee that includes representatives of government, industry and commerce, and the trade unions. They are announced annually on 21 April, the Queen's birthday. The applications are judged solely on merit. There is no allocation of awards for particular industries or region.

The scheme was originally devised during Labour Prime Minister Harold Wilson's first administration from October 1964 to April 1966. His campaign had included the slogan, 'the white heat of tech-nology', and it had become clear that UK industry was in danger of falling behind those of the USA and of the fast-reviving economies of war-ravaged Europe, as well as Japan. Furthermore, the pound sterling was under perennial pressure thanks to the UK's constant and growing trade gap in manufac-tured goods. Hence, the Queen's Award for Export Achievement was added.

To their delight, Stannah won the award for Export Achievement and three members of the company were invited to a reception at Buckingham Palace on 10 March 1988. It was suggested that as well as a Managing Director, representatives from the opera-tional side of the business and shop-floor should make up the trio. A ballot was held and the winners were Tony Rockey, a charge-hand in Stairlifts assembly, and Christine Harris, a senior clerk in trade and export sales order processing. Invitations were duly received from the Master of the Queen's Household and the three set off for London. Brian Stannah recorded the day:

6.12 In 1987, Stannah won a Queen's Award for Export Achievement. Here the Deputy Lord Lieutenant of Hampshire, Rear Admiral Sir Morgan Morgan-Giles, presents the award to Brian and Alan Stannah.

In recognition of the great importance of the occasion, we travelled 1st Class by train to London and by taxi from Waterloo to Buckingham Palace. In conjunction with our public relations consultant, we had arranged for a photographer to meet us at the Palace gates where we paid off the taxi and had our photos taken with the Palace railings and policemen as background. Dusk was drawing in. We then showed our passes and walked across the gravel fore-court, under the archway and across the large central forecourt which is normally hidden from view and finally arrived at the main entrance and red carpet which guided us up a gently ascending flight of stairs to a reception hallway. Here, our names were checked off and we had the opportunity to leave our coats. Together with the other arrivals, we then gently moved on up 2 further flights of shallow steps until we entered the main reception gallery. Whilst Police and uniformed Palace attendants were present, at no time was heavy security evident and the whole pro-cedure took place in a relaxed and gracious manner. Some 480 guests, together with I would estimate 40 or 50 Palace officials and members of the selection committees had collected in the main reception gallery. This was a chamber some 200 ft in length, with a high domed ceiling, rose coloured silk fabric walls and many priceless

6.13 Brian Stannah, Tony Rockey and Christine Harris at Buckingham Palace on 10 March 1988 to celebrate the company's Queen's Award.

paintings by such painters as Rubens, Rembrandt, Van Ruisdael and Cuyp. We all waited for about 10 minutes, during which time we chatted to people from other companies nearby and I was able to exchange comments with the Chairman of Cunard Limited, who of course do a lot of export business in terms of holidays on cruise ships sold to Americans, Japanese etc.

We had all been equipped with name-tags which were pinned on to our lapels and thus it was surprising to me when I was suddenly tapped on the shoulder and approached from behind by one of the Queen's equerries, who said, 'Ah – Mr Stannah, I have been looking for you. We will all be going in soon to be received by the Queen and Prince Philip and afterwards we will be distributed among several rooms. However, the Queen has said that she particularly wishes to meet you. Because there is quite a crush here, this may not be easy, so keep your eye open for me.' Imagine our amazement and excitement. Shortly after, the double doors at the far end of the reception hall opened and slowly there was forward movement which ultimately developed into a crocodile and then, one by one, we walked through the double doors and there, on our right, receiving the guests one by one were the Queen, Prince Philip and the Duke of Gloucester. It was a simple matter of a bow or curtsey, a handshake and a 'Good evening Ma'am', a handshake with Prince Philip who would make one short comment, and a handshake with the Duke of Gloucester, after which the guests gently moved on into one of the series of reception rooms where drinks were served and snacks were being passed around. We had our eye open for our Lieutenant Colonel, who appeared at our side within 2 or 3 minutes (many people must have arrived earlier, because although we arrived on time we were among the last in the line and thus the Queen only had a few more handshakes to complete before she was ready to circulate). We were gently asked to stand forward and to one side of the doorway through which we had just passed and then the Queen was with us. Briefly introduced to Tony, Christine and myself, she then spent 5 minutes with us, first asking about our company and products and then talking to Christine and Tony about their work. It was all very relaxed and natural and I was very impressed at her interest and at one point in the conversation her sense of humour. It was only afterwards, on the way home, that we heard the news about the skiing accident in which Prince Charles had been involved and over which she must have been very concerned only a short time before. The Queen then circulated on and we believe spoke to a number of other companies, although it can only have been a very small proportion of the 160 companies who were represented. I was talking to someone else and lost Christine and Tony for a while, but when I caught up with them I found them in animated conversation with the Duke of Gloucester who was participating fully and with great warmth and simplicity. The Prime Minister was present, but we did not get the opportunity to get close to her. Prince Philip was circulating in a genial way and hob-nobbing with one group after another. We had opportunity of circulating through the State reception rooms, all of which were magnificent with their wall coverings, lighting and chandeliers. At around 8.00 pm, it was clear that the reception would soon be drawing to a close and we accordingly withdrew and made our departure.

Christine, Tony and myself were invited as representatives of the whole workforce of the company and whilst we were present physically, we very much had in mind that the rest of the staff were with us in spirit, and in appreciating the honour of being able to attend we had the responsibility of sharing the experience afterwards with everyone else and I hope that this will be possible through briefing and perhaps in the next edition of *Elevation*. Whilst the surroundings in Buckingham Palace were impressive, to say the least, the affair was essentially informal. The Palace staff and the Queen's equerries were friendly and the Queen herself was simply attired in a woollen dress without noticeable jewellery and the reception was so well organised that everything was effortless.

We met some interesting people, including a local Basingstoke company who were unique because they have a total workforce of 4 including the M.D. and they export 95% of their product. They managed a 100% turn-out at the reception because the odd man out acted as chauffeur for the evening and apparently was well entertained downstairs in the Palace. A taxi outside the Palace gates and train home concluded the evening, which will be long remembered.

6.14 Alan Stannah presenting Douglas Bader with a cheque for Queen Mary's Hospital, Roehampton.

THE PERFORMANCE PLAN – SHARING IN THE GROWTH

Alan recalls:

> This started with a question from Brian to me: 'What are we doing about performance sharing with our employees?'
>
> This caused me to attend a couple of seminars on the subject, following which we appointed Douglas Bentley of Bentley Associates to introduce a scheme based on their theories of sharing any increase in the value added achieved through the trading operations of the company.
>
> The scheme, named our 'Performance Plan', was introduced in June 1980. Whether by coincidence or not, we had made a loss up to the end of May, but turned a profit in June allowing a Performance Plan payment of £13.88 to be made as shown on the first Performance Plan calculation sheet and, apart from only very occasional lapses, we have continued to do so thereafter.
>
> A booklet was produced explaining the mathematical complexities of the performance value added calculation on which the monthly payment was based. I suspect few people understood this.
>
> However, we became concerned that while the value added concept might work as a general principle, we might be one of the few for whom it did not. We decided to change to a straight share of profits based on the 20 per cent of profit that had been

achieved so far. This was distributed to employees as a regular payment, the only deductions being proportional to attendance – and has continued unchanged to this day.

The accompanying table shows that, to the end of 2016, over £54 million has been distributed under this enlightened scheme.

GROUP PERFORMANCE PLAN PAYOUTS

Year	Payout £000	Running total
1980 June	50 approx	50,000
81	100 approx	150,000
82	150 approx	300,000
83	200 approx	500,000
84	300 approx	800,000
85	416	1,216,000
86	662	1,878,000
87	724	2,602,000
88	767	3,369,000
89	1,057,393	4,426,000
90	1,090,7901	5,517,183
91	698,699	6,215,882
92	1,178,598	7,394,480
93	1,354,546	8,749,026
94	1,835,881	10,584,907
95	1,528,710	12,113,617
96	1,677,504	13,791,121
97	1,593,582	15,384,703
98	1,225,433	16,610,136
99	933,466	17,543,602
2000	1,175,858	18,719,460
2001	1,396,179	20,115,639
2002	1,874,702	21,990,341
2003	2,225,835	24,216,176
2004	2,217,548	26,433,724
2005	2,347,342	28,781,066
2006	1,831,864	30,612,930
2007	2,338,975	32,951,905
2008	2,139,401	35,091,306
2009	1,860,096	37,143,742
2010	2,021,044	39,164,786
2011	2,030,458	41,195,244
2012	2,275,411	43,470,655
2013	2,672,205	46,142,860
2014	2,896,818	49,039,678
2015	3,001,016	52,040,694
2016	2,409,095	54,449,789

Someone said to Brian Stannah recently: 'Does it not bother you that you and your brother would be £30 million better off if you hadn't set up that scheme?' Brian replied: 'Actually, I think we'd be worse off.'

Some companies operate an incentive scheme whereby individuals are rewarded as individuals for ideas that save the company money or improve its profitability. Stannah eschewed this approach as potentially counter-productive in that it tends to erode the teamwork ethos. Instead, Stannah set up what they call Performance Committees so that any employee with an idea can pass it to the Committee which will then discuss it and agree on what action should be taken. The resulting saving would then improve company per-

6.15 A very successful product for Stannah at this time was the range of Piccolo light passenger lifts.

formance and earnings, and *everyone* would benefit from a higher Performance Plan payout.

This was the composition of Stannah at the end of the 1980s:

Stannah Lifts Limited	A comprehensive range of low- to medium-rise passenger lifts having both traction and hydraulic drive in a range of sizes and with differing specifications to meet each of a number of specific market needs, including Homelifts, wheelchair lifts and the Piccolo light-duty passenger lifts.
Stannah Microlifts Limited	Non-passenger industrial and service lifts, each with the benefit of standard specifications, short delivery times and streamlined installation procedures.
Stannah Stairlifts Limited	Stairlifts, used by people with impaired mobility in their own home and also for wheelchair transportation in public and commercial buildings.
Stannah Special Lifts Limited	Individually designed to meet special projects and including major modernisations of existing installations – inclined lifts, lifts for marine applications and civil engineering structures are just three examples.
Stannah Lifts Services Limited	Providing Stannah's customers with after-care, and the expertise of this division extends to lifts of all other makes and types, including escalators.

Alan Stannah summarised the company's position by 1987:

> The Tylney Hall Overseas Distributors' Meeting and The Queen's Award for Export Achievement in 1987 were two landmark events that represented significant milestones in the history of the company.
>
> The Queen's Award for Export Achievement gave us recognition as a serious player in export markets and was a worthy recognition of all that had been done

over many years to build our markets and the products and production methods and administrative systems on which they were based.

Following this and the Tylney Hall ODM we could pause for breath after a hectic ride that had seen our company grow from its recovery after near bankruptcy in 1961 to a vibrant and expanding business. Computerised administrative and accounting systems provided a sound foundation and our factories had taken their first steps towards modern production methods and machine tools, with attractive new designs for both our lift cars and stairlifts from an internationally renowned design house. We had developed a vigorous service business throughout England and Wales and an active chain of Distributors for our stairlifts across much of the world.

6.16 Brian and Jenny Stannah presenting HRH Princess Anne
with a cheque for Riding for the Disabled in 1986.

Brian and Alan could then have decided that they had achieved enough and opted for an easy life, but that road was not for them, as they believed in continuing the tradition of the family business. There was more – indeed much more – to come.

6.17, 6.18 An example of Stannah's growing service and refurbishment business, this time at the London Clinic.

6.19, 6.20 And another example, this one at the Reader's Digest building.

CHAPTER SEVEN

Preface to Chapter Seven

Brian and Alan Stannah would like to make clear:

This book was inspired by the wish to record and preserve the history of the family business. It is a sad fact that so little is known of the company from the turn of the 20th century to the start of World War Two. We are fortunate that we know so much of events in earlier years and from the end of World War Two.

A warning – there is a danger in recording more recent history, the details are more copious and ruthless editing is needed to ensure that a reader in 50 and more years' time will experience a sense of balance throughout. Readers who are with the company at the time of publication may be disappointed, even slighted, by lack of mention. This chapter is thus a brief sketch of some of the essentials from around 1989. However, history will bring the right perspective and will, it is hoped, be set out in fuller detail when Volume 2 is written.

A Sketch of Recent Happenings – The 150 Years

IT'S A FAMILY BUSINESS

Stannah is, and always has been, a family business. That the family has managed to pass the business through five generations and that it is not only still growing but spreading itself throughout the world is a remarkable achievement. Passing over the reins for each generation is never easy and, at the end of the 1980s, Brian and Alan Stannah realised they must plan for the future and discussed at great length the future of their family business and what should be the way forward.

Brian said:

7.1 Brian Stannah – build a structure to safeguard the future.

Alan and I decided that the topic needed addressing and asked PE Consulting for their advice. PE proposed an experienced mentor with wide boardroom experience with whom, over some months, we discussed the issues. Our eventual decision was to try and prove that a different outcome from the ones he was suggesting existed, at least for the foreseeable future. We were the fourth generation in the business and blessed with five children between us. We shared the hope that among them there would be those keen and able to step into our shoes eventually so that the business could continue as a privately owned company. The strategy we adopted was to reduce the dependence of the business and its staff upon the two of us by stepping back from day-to-day responsibility while appointing Managing Directors who would run each part of the business. Derek Lloyd, who had joined as Service Director in 1984, was promoted to Managing Director of Stannah Lifts Services Limited and Duncan LeFeuvre, who was Managing Director of Stannah Microlifts Limited, also became Managing Director of Stannah Lifts Limited. In 1989 David Walton was recruited as Marketing and Operations Director of the Stairlifts business and Managing Director Designate (the Designate being quickly removed) as David filled the position that we had previously held. Together they joined Ian Ash, who had been appointed Finance Director in 1973 and with us formed what was later known as the Group Management Team (GMT).

So we now had the structure in place to safeguard the future of the company until the next generation might be considered for top jobs. A comment on nepotism is appropriate here. For a long time I thought nepotism is to be avoided at all costs. Nowadays I'm not so sure. Why? To answer that question one has to ask another one. Why run a family business? There are probably a number of reasons, depending upon each situation, but the overriding one is to give employment and job satisfaction to the family members. The business will be a reflection of what they are and what they are capable of. If they were to become passive shareholders not playing a part in the running of the business, it would probably function well, perhaps better than if they ran it themselves, but it would no longer be a true family business. This change would undoubtedly be detected by those touched by the business – staff, customers and suppliers. What is required is family involvement. This then flows down into the business as a whole with the staff and their dependants regarded as the wider family. The Stannahs are conscious that a staff approaching 2,000 (in August 2017) means that with their dependants probably in excess of 4,000 people rely on the business, a

7.2 Alan Stannah – with Brian – ensured their sons were in responsible positions within the company.

mantle of responsibility, just as the family rely on the staff fulfilling their various roles – a shared responsibility and a unique feature of a family business.

Alan has added:

We should recognise the magnitude of these changes. Although Brian and I retained the positions of Joint Chairmen and Directors of the operating companies, for the first time since the first Stannah family company was founded by Joseph Stannah in the 1860s, the day-to-day running lay outside the Stannah family. These appointments relieved the load on Brian and me enabling us to continue holding the reins. They also filled the gap until a further succession to our younger generation might be possible. They were indeed significant appointments that added considerable strength to the Group.

The Group Management function had evolved harmoniously and informally over the previous fifteen years but now a more formal structure was put in place with regular Group Board Meetings when we focused on the work being done to make progress in each individual area of company activities. As will be seen, these were wide-ranging and significant.

NEW BLOOD

While Brian and Alan had proved that they both had broad pairs of shoulders, the time had come when the loads had to be spread further. The new structure would not have been possible without sound financial controls which from the 1970s had progressively been put in place by the Group Financial Director, Ian Ash. Until 1984 he and Duncan LeFeuvre, the Managing Director of Microlifts, were Brian and Alan's second pair of shoulders. Then further top appointments were made by 1987 leading to a formal Group structure. The end of the 1980s saw the structure firmly established into Operating Divisions which were product-focused and coincidentally largely customer-focused. In due course people at the top retired, new appointments were made and the next generation (to be known as 5G) started to make their presence felt. The contributions made by those who led that dramatic growth must be recognised.

Ian Ash FCA was Group Financial Director from 1975 to 2006. When he succeeded Colin Wass in 1975 (who left to join the World Bank) Ian inherited financial

7.3 Ian Ash – Group Financial Director 1975–2006.

controls recorded in pen-and-ink. Had he joined even three years earlier, he would not have found controls, merely records, Colin's brief spell with the company having made a significant impact. Ian computerised the accounting systems and this caused a major wind of change, the first of many under his leadership. He knew the company was on a growth trajectory and that second-best would not be acceptable, so the wind of change blew for years and Ian acquired quite a 'hire and fire' reputation, but the result was a department staffed with competent and committed people resourced with efficient computerised systems.

He eventually managed the smooth transition with few hiccups to IBM's AS400 platform, one which with both regular upgrades and application enhancements would remain at the heart of the Group IT nerve centre to 2017 and beyond.

Brian and Alan and the next generation to work in the company had another reason to thank Ian. He acted as mentor to Jon and Patrick, the first two members of the fifth generation (known as 5G) to join the business, aiding and guiding their progress in their early years.

Brian and Alan would say that Ian's most significant claim to a permanent memorial was his gift for tight credit control and the support that this would give to the company doctrine of having NatWest Bank with them rather than the reverse, with independence from borrowed funds – and they would add that he was the most dependable and likeable of colleagues: 'Good personal chemistry.' However, more than that, Brian has reflected:

By the move to Andover in 1974, Pop, then 72, had essentially retired and the full weight of the business rested on the shoulders of Alan and me. I have asked myself if we felt the cold wind of exposure due to this responsibility and decided that no, we didn't. I then pondered on why this might have been and concluded that Ian, with his tight financial control and focus on credit control and cash flow, gave us this confidence. At that time we were a team of three and Ian continued to give his wholehearted support to the wider team following the new appointments through to his retirement in 2006.

Another great contributor to the growth of Stannah was Duncan LeFeuvre, who from its early days was Managing Director of Stannah Microlifts Limited, and of Stannah Lifts Limited from 1989 to 2007.

Duncan was a tireless worker, not a nine-to-five man, and one who devoted long days and perhaps nights in focusing on the detail of not just his businesses but a number of Group topics where he felt he could be of value. He was a loyal Stannah family man through and through. It was always clear where his loyalties lay. He had a broad pair of shoulders and was always ready and eager to take on Group-related tasks when they arose.

The formative years in Microlifts stood him in good stead when Marketing and Sales in Lifts became the key drivers in growing the business. The sales teams in both of his companies were highly effective, aided by his involvement in PR, promotion, print and publicity.

7.4 Duncan LeFeuvre – always showed clarity of thought.

Product development and continuous improvement were other key drivers both in product and in people terms. Duncan's technical team had the competence to innovate while also participating and leading the work of the various National and International Standards Committees. His people achieved and maintained Investors in People (IiP) accreditation, matching the steady increase in standards. Duncan also made an important contribution to Group Health and Safety policy development and implementation.

Duncan showed clarity of thought in running his businesses. The Blue Paper, later renamed The Stannah Blueprint, was one of Duncan's initiatives and is a lasting legacy to his creativity and commitment to the wider Group. He showed similar thought in supporting the family and the Group in the development of Group publicity and company culture.

Above all, Duncan was a good friend to so many and one of the family's right-hand men.

Duncan's initiative in understanding and responding to the market led to significant new product ranges. These were the Midilift for Machinery Directive platform lifts and the Goodsmaster range of goods-only lifts, both of which continued to be major planks within the Lifts businesses.

Duncan's health issues finally enforced his premature retirement in 2007 but not before he had supported Alastair Stannah's development and growing experience to the extent that he was appointed to step into Duncan's shoes as Managing

Director of Stannah Lifts Limited and Stannah Microlifts Limited. He left the legacy of a successful Microlifts business and a Lifts business poised to introduce new products to market.

Service back-up is all-important to a manufacturer and Derek Lloyd's appointment in 1984 is recalled by Alan Stannah as one of those happy business developments that, while not planned, had a significant and beneficial outcome. At that time the company was short of a Branch Manager in Birmingham and Derek made contact with the company to see what this might entail. Brian arranged for Derek to visit Andover, when they struck up an immediate rapport and Brian said, 'Never mind Branch Manager, how about Service Division Director?' Derek was pleased to accept this position and brought a welcome rigour and discipline in his control and development of the Service Branch network, with a tight grip on cost control. At that time there were too many red numbers against the Branch accounts and as the months passed there was a steady trend of red to black with a welcome contribution to Group earnings and cash-flow.

Derek's appointment as Managing Director of Stannah Lifts Services Limited and position on the GMT in 1989 was a worthy recognition of this improved performance.

When Jon Stannah joined the Service Division in 1987 he was fortunate to have Derek as his mentor until Derek's retirement in 1997. Thanks to Derek's good guidance and example, Jon was able to take over the reins as Managing Director of Stannah Lifts Services Limited.

Derek left a legacy of a sound and well-run network of Service Branches stretching from the south coast to Scotland, for which he could be justly proud.

When the need for new blood in Stairlifts was identified, David Walton was recruited in 1989.

Born and brought up in South Africa, he had graduated from New College, Oxford, after coming to the university as a Rhodes Scholar. He had qualified as an accountant with Arthur Andersen in the City and then returned to Africa to run a factory for the battery company, Chloride. He then joined the dynamic American company, Abbott Laboratories, voted during his time there as the best-managed company in the USA by the influential *Forbes* magazine.

David spent eighteen years in the business and had a huge influence on its growth. Key areas of his focus were product development, market development and Continuous Improvement. With the accountant's mind and a disciplined approach, he had a measured way of analysing wants and creating action plans.

An early initiative of David Walton's was the introduction of Continuous Improvement, which created a new 'can do' spirit in the organisation and helped enable the staff to realise their potential. Productivity gains resulted.

Export activity grew apace, aided by continued development of the Distributor network and the regular Distributor Meetings to unveil new products. Acquisitions were made and markets entered. Relationships were further developed, notably with family businesses Lifta in Germany and Chuo in Japan. Wholly owned subsidiaries were created or acquired in France, Belgium, Italy, Holland, USA, Slovakia and Ireland.

Awards followed: the second and third Queen's Awards for Export Achievement in 1994 and 1999, Best Factory Award in 2003 (the subsequent and previous winner being Nissan), a Golden Trophy Design Award in 2005 and the fourth Queen's Award for Enterprise – International Trade in 2010. While new product introduction took longer, a steady stream of new and incrementally improved products were brought to market despite a more rigorous approach to life-testing which put a brake on things but would minimise the costly recalls of product-in-service.

David Walton, with his early background in accountancy, ran a tight ship, speaking the same language as Ian Ash's Finance Department.

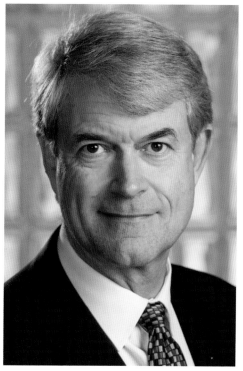

7.5 David Walton ran a tight ship.

SUCCESSION

So, thus far the chain of succession is clear – Joseph, Albert, Leslie ('Pop'), Brian and Alan, all Stannahs so far, then joined with Messrs Ash, LeFeuvre, Lloyd and Walton to form a team of six. However, time would pass. Those four fortuitous appointments of Ash, LeFeuvre, Lloyd and Walton eventually ran their course and grateful goodbyes were said in 1997, 2006, 2007 and 2008. If 'Pop' could have looked into the future he would have seen that the fruits of his marriage with Jean would eventually result in a 'tribe' of over 30 sons and daughters, their spouses and their offspring, Brian with three sons (Jon, Patrick and Nick) and Alan with a son and a daughter (Alastair and Helen). Would Pop have envisaged that a new cast could be ready and waiting in the wings? We'll never know.

Much change in a short period and who to fill the shoes?

We now move into the final ten years because 2017 will mark 150 years and publication. This chapter started with a warning and thus brevity has been the need, with the key players and their parts just lightly sketched in.

The period in question included a world recession sparked by injudicious lending by UK and American banks. Commercial life became harder from 2007 and the four or so years that followed. The company not only survived but prospered, although Lifts bore the brunt of the downturn with its reliance on the UK construction industry.

THE SUCCESSORS

Prior to the retirement of Directors between 1997 and 2008 the top Board GMT, as we have seen, had comprised Brian and Alan, together with Ian Ash, Duncan LeFeuvre, Derek Lloyd and David Walton. After the retirements, the GMT was composed of Brian and Alan, Jon (Services), Alastair (Lifts and Microlifts), Mike Howe and Tim Eagles (Stairlifts), Patrick (UK Stairlift Distribution), Debi Coveney (Group Financial Director), later joined by Martin Carter (Group Operations Director), and most recently Nick (running Stairlifts International Sales) and Pete Perry (Managing Director – Maintenance and Repair Division) who, for many years, had supported Jon in Services with responsibility for Major Projects, Escalators and Walkways and the Service Branches.

From around 2014 Brian and Alan progressively would withdraw from the GMT, their main roles being to lead the Family Board which would meet regularly to control Group assets and sanction the direction of the businesses.

More recent developments in the period included:

Lifts and Microlifts – Efforts were focused on improving and expanding the product range to meet the needs of more of the market and support the ambition to grow the business. While this continued, the Lifts business also had to get through the financial crisis of 2007–2008 and the subsequent recession. This had a significant impact on the lift market which took some years to recover – and in 2012 Lifts took the difficult decision to cease manufacture of passenger lifts, with the last lift made in November 2013. The rationale for this decision was two-fold. Firstly, passenger lifts would be sourced from leading European manufacturers with far greater scale and a much wider range enabling Lifts to enter new areas of the market previously out of reach. Secondly, it was to enable Lifts' design and manufacturing team to concentrate on the development of the Midilift range of vertical platform lifts, leading to various improvements and new products being launched. A new Homelift is being developed for launch in 2018 to further extend the range. Microlifts also expanded its offering, working with both Daldoss (the partnership passing the 40-year mark) and also other suppliers to grow its range of larger goods lifts.

Services – The ten year contract with Network Rail was retained for a further ten years and along with steady growth the lift and stairlift service portfolio grew to over 90,000 units. Due to the scale of the bespoke lift work with Network Rail and other customers with special requirements a Major Projects Division was established. To date they have installed 563 passenger lifts alone on railway stations across the UK. A move into escalators and walkways in 2007 followed after an approach from the Chinese manufacturer Anlev and this provided welcome growth during the financial crisis, allowing the Group to compete for both new and service work from customers with a wider range of lift equipment. The out-of-hours customer service (previously switched over to a supplier in the evenings and weekends) was brought in-house, ensuring customers could talk directly to a Stannah employee and receive assistance at any time of the day – 365 days a year.

Stairlifts – A succession of new and improved products continued to be launched including the 600 model – a new generation straight stairlift, a range of chairs available on straight and curved stairlifts – the Starla and the Siena. Also, a uniquely designed perch-on chair – the Sadler. The next generation single tubed curved stairlift was launched towards the end of 2017 and a suite of digital services have been developed to support users, including the Connect app (to provide peace of mind to relatives and friends). Our markets continued to expand through both organic growth coming from stairlift sales, but also increasingly from sales of homelifts and vertical and inclined platform lifts. Further expansion continued with acquisitions in Norway, Portugal and Spain and a new subsidiary in Canada.

7.6 The Stannah Group Management Team 2017.

Stannah Management Services – A major investment in an in-house open source integrated Group-wide IT system will provide the foundation for our processes for many years to come. A Group HR function now supports all our businesses (both in the UK and overseas) and a comprehensive Fleet Management system that uses state-of-the-art technology was installed across all of our fleet vehicles in the UK. Our finance team has developed to support all our international activity (including acquisitions) and continues to ensure our financial independence by managing our growing range of financial and property investments.

VISIT BY HRH THE PRINCE OF WALES

One event which justifies the fullest coverage is the visit by HRH The Prince of Wales to the company's Head Office at Andover in February 2011.

The visit was in recognition of Stannah's status as a successful, family-owned British manufacturer that had grown through five generations and was a substantial employer and exporter. It was also to celebrate the production of the company's 500,000th stairlift and followed a Queen's Award for Enterprise – International Trade in 2010 to Stairlifts.

Following the visit, a letter was received from Jonathan Hellewell, the Prince's Assistant Private Secretary, saying:

> His Royal Highness was tremendously impressed by Stannah and by your wonder-ful employees and has asked me to pass on his thanks and praise to you. The Prince was immensely touched, both by the warm welcome he received and your very generous gift of the two stairlifts to Abbeyfield and to the Almshouse Association. [Almshouses have existed for over 1,000 years, enabling individuals in need to retain their independence and to live in the local community, while Abbeyfield is a not-for-profit organisation dedicated to making the lives of older people easier and more fulfilling.]

When at the time Jonathan Sibun of *The Daily Telegraph* interviewed Managing Director Jon Stannah, he gave some revealing answers to his questions.

He said that the company was run by a family board made up of two septua-genarian Joint-Chairmen from the fourth generation and four of their five chil-dren. When asked what happened when there was a disagreement, he said:

> We thrash it out and have always been able to. There's something about the values of the business and the way we've been brought up that means we're all of a quite a similar school of thought.

Noting that, at that time, the company sold into 42 countries and had ten overseas subsidiaries, including a hub in the USA which Stannah cited as an example of the benefits of private ownership, Jon Stannah continued:

7.7 Jon Stannah with HRH The Prince of Wales.

We probably wouldn't still be operating in the US (often referred to as the graveyard of UK companies setting up there) if we were public, because it took years for that business to move into the volumes and profitability that would have satisfied a publicly quoted company. It was our first subsidiary outside Europe and there was a lot of uncertainty about whether we were stretching ourselves too far. It would have been easy to make a knee-jerk decision and decide we weren't making the returns we needed.

The royal visit was reported extensively, with a number of photographs in the French magazine, *Le Figaro*. The article concluded with: *Le credo de l'equipe Stannah – 'Nous prenons soin de vous'* [The Stannah company slogan – 'We take care of you'].

7.8 (overleaf, top) The Stannah Family with HRH The Prince of Wales.
7.9 (overleaf, bottom) HRH The Prince of Wales with Stannah employees and guests.

7.10 HRH The Prince of Wales with Brian, Alan and Jon Stannah.

ANOTHER CELEBRATION

Monday, 15 June 2015 saw the car park at Andover covered in marquees. The occasion marked 40 years of stairlift manufacture and was to say a big 'thank you' to the many staff who had helped to make that possible. A sit-down barbeque and hog roast lunch, competitions, music, fun and games together with the odd speech combined to create a happy party for the wider 'Stannah Family', including visitors from company offices in the USA, Italy, Spain, Czech Republic, Slovakia, France and Belgium.

KEEP IT IN THE FAMILY

Above all, the Stannahs are a closely knit family, each understanding the commitment necessary to maintain the momentum of the business.

There is a thread of sailing that runs through the family, from old photos of Albert with Leslie and Colin on holiday on the Norfolk Broads, through Leslie where pre-war yachting prepared him for rapid commissioning as a Sub-Lieutenant

7.11 Alan's Solent Sunbeam V46 Spray – with Jackie crewing during Cowes Week.

RNVR in 1939, to Brian's varied succession of yachts and Alan's lifelong and widespread sailing activities [see photo] that continue to this day in his beloved racing keelboat, Solent Sunbeam V46 Spray. Also more recently the varied exploits of 5G (both Patrick and Nick Stannah having raced in the Fastnet). Navigating the course of the family business is clearly second nature. Alan's sailing and yacht racing has been a lifelong activity that continues to this day, for many years with Jackie as a valued crew member including bucketing and bailing around many a rough Cowes Week race.

How do the Stannahs expect their successful firm to continue as a family business? In an interview for *Real Business* magazine, Brian Stannah said:

Try to prepare in advance. Get the culture cast in stone, then, if it ain't broke, don't try to fix it. Set high standards in all that you do and remember that your number one resource in your business is your people. Don't talk about profits, talk about earnings. And whatever you do don't sell the company. The latter point is critical. The truth is that companies often do better under family ownership [a recent survey of family businesses by *Forbes* magazine in the USA confirmed this point], which encourages stability, long-term thinking and loyalty from staff. Selling off the firm can be like selling the family silver – trading an investment for future generations. If it's healthy, it's worth more than whatever you'll swap it into. Your asset base will then decline and you'll completely lose control of how those assets grow.

In terms of succession, Brian and Alan believe it should be gradual:

> Ideally, it's something that should take place over a period of time. You should start the process sooner than you might wish and end it later than your successors might wish.

By the end of 2007, Brian and Alan Stannah had ensured that their sons were in responsible positions within the Stannah Group. They had also ensured that they had all arrived there after experience elsewhere in the business world and/or a number of posts within the Stannah Group itself.

BLUEPRINT

The thread which has run through the business during its 150 years is 'integrity'. A dictionary has defined this as 'the quality of honesty and having strong moral principles'. This was first set down by Joseph in his 'Rules of Life'.

The word 'blueprint' may not be familiar to today's reader. It was familiar to Leslie Stannah when he was given the business by Albert on returning home from the Royal Navy at the end of the Second World War. The lifetime inheritance consisted of a pile of bricks, the remains of the bomb-damaged factory at Tiverton Street, Elephant and Castle in south-east London and a roll of 'blueprints'. Back to the dictionary – 'a blueprint is a reproduction of a technical drawing using a contact print process on light sensitive sheets, first introduced in the 19th century, having white lines and text on a blue ground'. Today that bit of history is honoured and remembered in the family's guidance document for the company – 'Blueprint'. It would restate them to ensure that the integrity with which the business had been run would be sustained for the future. Key words would be 'ethical' and 'responsible'. It would embrace the main areas of responsibility that permeate down from the Directors to all levels in the company. It would be the anchor point of how the business is to be run and importantly be available to all, giving guidance as to the expectations of the family. It would be a 'blueprint' for the future and would be so named.

For some 30 years the company's brand identity employed its Bird logo. Implying a sense of freedom, it particularly resonated with the company's stairlift customers although its fresh approach was liked by the commercial sector. However, in 2010 Stannah felt they needed to strengthen their identity and that this should be combined with and embody a restatement of their core principles and beliefs. The Blue Paper which had been in use for more than twenty years was updated following a deep analysis of those principles and beliefs. The outcome was an amalgam/combination of a new mission statement based on 'We take care', a set of guidance principles set out in 'Blueprint', and a new logo in a bold but simple typeface featuring the Stannah name, by now well known, as a stand-alone icon with a streamlined 'bird' as a supporting image.

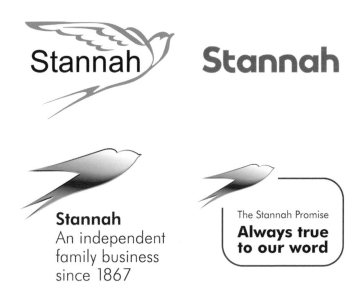

7.12 Stannah combined logo, Heritage and Our Promise logos.

'Blueprint' previously covered Ambition and Values, Health, Safety and the Environment, Our Customers and People, Our Brand, Business Strategy, Product Development, Sales and Distribution, Systems and Processes, Financing, Procurement, Assets and Welfare. During 2017 the 'Blueprint 150' document was produced.

Would the company be as it is today, still family-owned and in a substantial way of business and free of debt, without Joseph Stannah's 'Rules of Life'? Will these principles be sustained so that Volume 2 may be born in years to come? Let us hope so.

BACK TO FIRST PRINCIPLES

Leslie ('Pop') and Jean were married in 1927. Brian and Alan, the fourth generation (or 4G), were born, grew up and married Jenny in 1963 and Jackie in 1968 respectively. Three sons, Jonathan, Patrick and Nicholas, and a son and daughter, Alastair and Helen, followed (all now referred to as 5G). All are now in the business, Helen having started permanent employment in the HR Department in 2016 after a long course of studies which have resulted in BSCs in Occupational Therapy and Physiotherapy and an MSc in Applied Ergonomics and Human Factors. Marriage to Jim Stirrup, now a Consultant Cardiac Specialist, resulted in daughters Freya and twins Phoebe and Emily who with Jon and Ceri's Sam, Olivia, James, Sasha and Beth, Patrick's Louis, Barnaby and Sebastian, Alastair and Esther's Layla, Ivor, and twins Sid and Betty and Nick and Andrea's Reuben, Clara and Henry (the eleventh) together form 6G. From Pop to Jean down the family tree to eighteen in two generations – quite an achievement. Wouldn't they be proud!

7.13 Alastair, Jon, Helen, Nick and Patrick – all now referred to as 5G.

ALAN'S CLOSING TRIBUTE – '150 YEARS'

As we draw this edition of the Stannah history book to its close, I would like to reflect on all those with whom I have worked in the development and running of our company over these many years.

I will initially only mention one by name – my brother Brian, who has held a leading role at Stannah in all my time at our company and for some years before that.

Without Brian's steady hand alongside Pop in our early troubled times I would likely not have had a company to join when I completed my time as an engineering trainee at Hammond and Champness Lifts Ltd in 1963. In guiding our direction through the early days of our nationwide Service Branch network and towards and through the development of our UK and export stairlift business, Brian set the foundations for the growth and success that was to follow, in which he has continued to play his full part. However, none of this would have been possible without the many and widespread contributions from a changing cast of work colleagues at all levels throughout our company who have given their efforts and contributions over so many years.

These range from our most able Financial and Managing Directors and Directors, both family and non-family, and their supporting management and operational teams. We truly understand the value of all they have brought to Stannah and, above all, we as a family have enjoyed their company – all of which continues with our present team today and we trust will continue for long in the future.

We have seen many changes since the days when we were based in a small workshop in Tiverton Street in London and to everyone who has made this possible I give my sincere thanks.

It is a particular pleasure to see that we have Jon, Patrick, Alastair and Nick Stannah (members of the next generation) working within the company in leading roles – recently joined by Alastair's sister, Helen Stirrup. We thank all of those who have welcomed each in turn as they have joined us and helped them find their feet and guided them to their present positions.

Time is moving on and we are delighted to see we are now benefitting from the first inputs to our company from Sam Stannah, representing the next generation of our family – which between Stannah and Stirrup extends to a cast of eighteen young people who we hope will ensure continued family involvement for many years into the future.

We are also very pleased to be a family company in a wider sense, in that many of those who work with us have their family members working also with us as part of the Stannah team – and long may this continue as a welcome characteristic of our company.

My own time in our family business, which now extends to over 50 years, has been made so much easier by the steadfast support I have received from my wife Jackie over these years. Truly a rock that has given me stability and good companionship in all we have done together – from raising our family to sailing and skiing and not least in preparing my daily sandwich lunches which in number will soon be approaching 10,000! Fortunately I quite like Jackie's rolls and sandwiches.

We can all be proud that the services and products we provide for our customers bring real value to their lives. As a company that has shown continued growth for over 50 years, we can also take satisfaction in what this has meant for our country's economy in growing employment, the quality of our goods and services and our widespread training programmes and career development.

There is nothing so satisfying in developing the growth of a company as seeing a new product or business proposal evolve from a flickering flame that can be lost through a single discouraging word, through all the stages of development to a thriving business venture bringing growing employment opportunities to the communities in which our operations are based. We are privileged to have the opportunity to support such developments – and, through them, the strength and vitality of our communities and our country.

BRIAN'S CLOSING REMARKS

Alan has used kind words about me and then written on behalf of both of us. I would like to add comment on the value that Alan has brought to the business. Not named as such, but apart from his roles as Joint Managing Director and then Joint Chairman he has fulfilled the role of Chief Engineer for very many years. He has maintained the highest possible standards of engineering, integrity and product safety and rose to the challenges of leading the manufacturing functions of Lifts and Stairlifts until 1988/9 when thereafter as unnamed Chief Engineer he has held the reins until this day. We owe him an enormous debt of gratitude. Champion of training apprenticeships, further education and singer of praises of engineering in the classroom are further areas of Alan's influence. One can truly say he casts a long shadow.

Also we both must be grateful to Jon, Patrick, Alastair, Nick and Helen who in 2017 are now as a team at the helm and for the contributions each has made. Jon (now Group Managing Director) has 30 years under his belt with the others hard on his heels and all keeping the ship on an even keel and floating high on the water.

The introduction of this Epilogue contained a warning. Ruthless editing has been necessary and a deliberate decision has been made not to succumb to the strong temptation to feature the key players of today's business. Their time will come in volume two and we have a plan for that in the not too distant future.

When I joined Pop the staff numbered about 24, and not many more four years later when Alan came on board. Together we have seen the number increase to 1,900-plus (in August 2017). We considered listing each and every member of the wider family by name as an appendix, but Data Protection law has not made it practical. The success of the company is due in great measure to the quality of the many who in their widely differing ways, using their knowledge, skill and behaviour to best advantage, succeeded in satisfying the customers without whom there would be no family business. To each and every one, from the family, an enormous 'Thank You' for the 150 years from 1867 to 2017.

Afterword

On 1 June 2017 it was announced that Brian and Alan Stannah had both been awarded an MBE (Member of the Most Excellent Order of the British Empire) in the Queen's Birthday Honours List.

This made a perfect coincidence in that it was in the same year that the family company was celebrating its 150th anniversary and in particular remembering the efforts and achievements of our founder Joseph Stannah.

Joseph had the insight and vision to recognise the need for vertical transportation in buildings and created a lift company in Victorian London in 1867. Future generations of the Stannah family built on this legacy, and this award recognises the achievement of Brian and Alan in transforming a small family business into a large international company.

The two brothers grew the business from a turnover of about £35,000 and a workforce of just 24 employees in the early 1960s to a turnover approaching £250 million and employees numbering nearly 2,000 in 2017.

A significant achievement of the two brothers was to realise, and capitalise on, the promise of the stairlift in the 1970s. Of course, there are competitors, but Brian and Alan have made sure that the Stannah Stairlifts are of the highest quality so that Stannah is now a household name, so that if you say 'Stannah' to anyone the reply is always, 'Oh, yes, they make stairlifts, don't they?'

Not only stairlifts, of course. The lift business continued to diversify and grow, demonstrating that while our lift engineering skills had underpinned our success in stairlifts they were still very relevant in the world of commercial lifts.

Brian and Alan have always valued their people and have considered them part of a wider family and were keen to ensure employees shared in the financial success of the company. In 1980 they set up a Performance Plan. This very enlightened scheme meant that 20 per cent of profits were awarded to all employees and from 1980 to 2016 over £50 million has been distributed.

The two brothers can also be very proud of the export achievements of the business which have earned them four Queen's Awards since 1987. Not only has this been a significant contributor to the company's growth, it has also provided a useful contribution to the UK economy's balance of trade figures.

Brian and Alan Stannah receiving their MBEs from HRH The Prince of Wales.

Alan and Brian Stannah with their MBEs outside Buckingham Palace.

Asked to comment, Brian and Alan said:

We are proud to be the recipients of such an honour and to accept it on behalf of past and present family members and all the employees who have contributed to our success over the last 150 years. A steadfast commitment to innovation, quality and customer service have been the guiding principles of our family business and are as relevant today as they were when we joined the business. Our hard working and loyal colleagues have been integral to upholding these values over the years, and to them we are very grateful.

Brian and Alan, the fourth generation of the family business, have also put in a great effort to bring on and encourage the fifth generation so that Jon, Patrick, Alastair, Nick and Helen are all in responsible positions and making an enormous contribution to the continued growth of the family business.

BIBLIOGRAPHY

Ackroyd, Peter, *London, The Biography*, Chatto & Windus, 2000
Addison, Paul, *No Turning Back*, Oxford University Press, 2010

Bailey, Paul, *The Oxford Book of London*, Oxford University Press, 1995
Barnett, Correlli, *British Dreams 1945–50*, Macmillan, 1995
Barnett, Correlli, *The Verdict of Peace*, Macmillan, 1988
Bower, Tom, *Maxwell the Outsider*, Mandarin, 1988
Brendon, Piers, *Decline and Fall of the British Empire*, Jonathan Cape, 2007
Brown, George, *In My Way*, Victor Gollancz, 1971
Burgess, Eleanor and Mary Rounce (eds), *Boreham – History, Tales and Memories of an Essex Village*, self-published

Clark, Alan, *The Tories*, Weidenfeld & Nicolson, 1998

Day, Sir Robin, *… But With Respect*, Weidenfeld & Nicholson, 1993
Dimbleby, Jonathan, *Richard Dimbleby*, Hodder & Stoughton, 1975
Dugan, Emily, *Finding Home*, Icon Books, 2015

Eden, Sir Anthony, *Full Circle*, Cassell, 1960
Ensor, Sir Robert, *England 1870–1914*, Oxford University Press 1936
Evans, Harold, *Good Times, Bad Times*, Atheneum, 1984

Frost, David, *Autobiography*, Harper Collins, 1993

Gardner, Juliet, *The Thirties*, Harper Press, 2010
Gilbert, Martin, *The Twentieth Century 1900–1933*, HarperCollins 1997
Gilbert, Martin, *The Twentieth Century 1933–1951*, HarperCollins 1998
Gilbert, Martin, *The Twentieth Century 1952–1999*, HarperCollins 1999

Harris, Robin, *The Conservatives*, Bantam Press, 2011
Hattersley, Roy, *Fifty Years On*, Little Brown, 1997
Heath, Edward, *The Course of My Life*, Coronet Books, 1998
Hennessy, Peter, *Never Again*, Jonathan Cape, 1992
Hennessy, Peter, *Having it so Good*, Allen Lane, 2006
Hobsbawm, Eric, *Age of Extremes*, Michael Joseph, 1994
Hoffman, David, *The Dead Hand*, Icon Books, 2009

Hutber, Patrick, *The Decline and Fall of the Middle Class*, Penguin, 1977
Hutton, Will, *The State We're In*, Jonathan Cape, 1995

James, Lawrence, *The Middle Class*, Little Brown, 2006
Jeal, Tim, *Baden-Powell*, Pimlico, 1989

Keegan, John, *The Second World War*, Pimlico, 1997
Kynaston, David, *Austerity Britain 1945–51*, Bloomsbury, 2007
Kynaston, David, *Family Britain 1951–57*, Walker, 2009

Lacqueur, Walter, *Europe Since Hitler: The Rebirth of Europe*, Penguin, 1972
Laybourn, Keith, *Britain on the Breadline*, Sutton Publishing, 1990

MacDonald, John, *Francis Frith's Around Andover*, Frith, 2001
Marr, Andrew, *History of Modern Britain*, Pan Books, 2008
Marwick, Arthur, *Britain in Our Century*, Thames & Hudson, 1984
Morgan, Kenneth, *The People's Peace*, Oxford University Press, 1990

Naughtie, James, *The New Elizabethans*, Collins, 2012

Paxman, Jeremy, *Friends in High Places*, Michael Joseph, 1990
Petersen, L.A., *Otis Elevator Company, The First 100 Years*, self-published
Porter, Roy, *London, a Social History*, Hamish Hamilton, 1996

Ryle, Sarah, *The Making of Tesco*, Bantam Press, 2013

Sandbrook, Dominic, *Never Had It So Good*, Little Brown, 2005
Sandbrook, Dominic, *White Heat*, Little Brown, 2006
Seldon, Anthony, *Blair Unbound*, Pocket Books, 2007
Sewell, Gordon, *The Story of Parkhouse and Wyatt*, self-published
Skidelsky, Robert, *John Maynard Keynes*, Macmillan, 1992
Sturgeon, William (publisher), *Elevator World, October 1982: A Celebration*, self-published

Thelfall, Kevin, *One Stop, One Life*, Icon Books, 2014
Timmins, Nicholas, *The Five Giants*, Harper Collins, 1995

Vinen, Richard, *Thatcher's Britain*, Pocket Books, 2010

Young, Hugo, *This Blessed Plot*, Macmillan, 1998
Young, Hugo, *One of Us*, Pan Macmillan, 1990

Ziegler, Philip, *Edward Heath*, Harper Press, 2010

INDEX